T0301493

# Spatial Scenarios in a Global Perspective

NEW HORIZONS IN REGIONAL SCIENCE

**Series Editor:** Philip McCann, *Professor of Economic Geography, University of Groningen, The Netherlands and Professor of Economics, University of Waikato, New Zealand*

Regional science analyses important issues surrounding the growth and development of urban and regional systems and is emerging as a major social science discipline. This series provides an invaluable forum for the publication of high quality scholarly work on urban and regional studies, industrial location economics, transport systems, economic geography and networks.

*New Horizons in Regional Science* aims to publish the best work by economists, geographers, urban and regional planners and other researchers from throughout the world. It is intended to serve a wide readership including academics, students and policymakers.

Titles in the series include:

# Spatial Scenarios in a Global Perspective

Europe and the Latin Arc Countries

*Edited by*

Roberto Camagni

*Professor of Urban Economics, Politecnico di Milano, Italy*

Roberta Capello

*Professor of Regional Economics, Politecnico di Milano, Italy*

NEW HORIZONS IN REGIONAL SCIENCE

**Edward Elgar**

Cheltenham, UK • Northampton, MA, USA

Published by
Edward Elgar Publishing Limited
The Lypiatts
15 Lansdown Road
Cheltenham
Glos GL50 2JA
UK

Edward Elgar Publishing, Inc.
William Pratt House
9 Dewey Court
Northampton
Massachusetts 01060
USA

A catalogue record for this book
is available from the British Library

Library of Congress Control Number: 2011929465

ISBN  978 0 85793 561 8

Typeset by Servis Filmsetting Ltd, Stockport, Cheshire
Printed and bound by MPG Books Group, UK

# Contents

# Contributors

**Antonio Affuso** has been an official at the Italian Ministry of Economy and Finance, State General Accounting Department, Departmental Study Service (Se.S.D.) since December 2010. Formerly he was a research fellow in regional economics at the Politenico of Milan.

**Rafael Boix** is a lecturer in the Department of Economic Structure, Universitat de València, Spain, and a member of the editorial board of *Sviluppo Locale*. Formerly he was an external consultant for the OECD and undertook applied research for the Spanish Ministry of Industry, Barcelona province government, and Barcelona City Hall.

**Roberto Camagni** is Professor in Urban Economics and Economic Assessment of Urban Transformation at the Politecnico of Milan, Italy. He is Past-President of the European Regional Science Association (ERSA), and was Head of the Department for Urban Affairs at the Presidency of the Council of Ministers, Rome, under the first Prodi government, 1997–98. He is the author of many scientific papers and a textbook in urban economics, published in Italian, French and Spanish.

**Roberta Capello** is Professor in Regional Economics at the Politecnico of Milan, Italy. She is Past-President of the Regional Science Association International (RSAI), editor in chief of the Italian *Journal of Regional Science* and co-editor of *Letters in Spatial and Resource Science* (Springer Verlag). She is the author of many scientific papers and a textbook in regional economics, published in Italian and English.

**Ugo Fratesi** has been Associate Professor in Regional and Urban Economics at the Politecnico of Milan, Italy since January 2011, and a member of the editorial board and book review editor of the Italian *Journal of Regional Science* since 2008. He is the author of two books and several papers published in refereed journals in the field of regional economics.

**Vittorio Galletto** is Senior Economist at the Barcelona Institute of Regional and Urban Studies (IERMB), Spain. Formerly he was an associate professor and researcher at the Department of Applied Economics, Universitat Autònoma de Barcelona and an employee in a private consulting firm specializing in regional development.

*Spatial scenarios in a global perspective*

**Jacques Robert** is the director of TERSYN (Agence Européenne 'Territoires et Synergies') in Strasbourg, France. He is an expert in European territorial development issues and advises European as well as national and regional institutions, and is the author of numerous reports and papers.

**Joan Trullén** is Professor Titular of Regional and Urban Economics (Universitat Autònoma de Barcelona), Spain and since 2009, Director of IERMB (Institut d'Estudis Regionals i Metropolitans de Barcelona). He was commissioned by the Mayor of Barcelona for the Barcelona Knowledge Project (1997–2004), and was General Secretary of Industry for the Spanish government (2004–08). He has published in the field of local economic development, urban policies and industrial districts.

# 1. Building local after-crisis scenarios in a global perspective

**Roberto Camagni and Roberta Capello**

## 1.1 THE REASONS FOR A LOCAL AFTER-CRISIS SCENARIO EXERCISE

Far-seeing economic scenario building and forecasting have always been important exercises to guide policy makers in the construction of anticipatory policies. Such exercises become all the more important in a period of severe economic downturns, in which different reactions by economic systems to turbulence give rise to completely different economic scenarios, each requiring different policy interventions at all territorial levels.

The difficulty and responsibility of choosing development policies becomes more complicated at local level. While – as today widely accepted by the most advanced literature on the subject – long-term development is largely a supply-side phenomenon based on general rules and institutional frames, but above all nourished by the internal entrepreneurial capabilities of regions and places and by the local capacity to exploit existing resources efficiently, local policies require detailed knowledge of local resources and potentials. In fact, the possibility for any region to contribute to the general EU growth strategy depends on the creative exploitation of its own assets of territorial capital; their preservation, completion and enrichment by setting appropriate priorities to local and regional policies; and the 'tapping' and mobilization of previously 'untapped' resources.

If this endeavour is already somewhat complicated, it becomes even more difficult in periods of economic crisis, when structural, long-term and supply policies have to cope and integrate with short-term, demand policies, and when an overall scarcity of public resources must be complemented by private resources. Achievement of the necessary goals of increased efficiency, innovativeness and competitiveness requires difficult processes of activity reallocation among sectors, the faster introduction of technological progress, and the assumption of new risks linked to new production fields – all of which processes are difficult to carry out in conditions of employment stress and a shortage of public resources.

For all these reasons, an exercise aimed at building after-crisis scenarios with a methodology able to merge global driving forces and trends with the local potentials and assets of each province in Europe is of paramount importance. The present book represents a second, and more advanced, development of ideas first discussed in a research programme undertaken as part of an ESPON (European Spatial Observation Network) project developed in the 2008–09 period.[1] Its main goals are interesting and rather ambitious: to build new, after-crisis scenarios for European regions; to devise new methodologies and tools to support policy makers in quantitative assessment (of past trends) and foresight (of the new potential ones); and finally, as interestingly requested by the ESPON Coordination Unit, to develop a stimulating partnership process between scholars, local–regional policy makers and European officials in charge of EU regional policy. The results achieved bear witness that these goals have largely been accomplished: after-crisis scenarios have been devised, building on a previous ESPON experience (Part I); a new methodology and a new econometric tool have been created (Part II); an interesting picture of different and alternative after-crisis territorial development paths is provided for a case study area, the Latin Arc countries (Spain, France and Italy) and the Latin Arc provinces network, running along the Mediterranean coast, with a final zoom-in on the province of Barcelona (Part III); finally, local and regional policy recommendations are made, building on the scenario results and made possible by close cooperation and interaction between scientists and local policy makers (Part IV).

All these achievements have required the solution of conceptual and methodological problems related mainly to the creation of global, top-down, after-crisis scenarios consistent with the local, bottom-up, development potentials of each single territory. The main conceptual and methodological innovative efforts are described in what follows.

---

[1]  The first ideas were developed within the ESPON 2013 'targeted' project concerning 'Spatial Scenarios: new tools for local and regional territories', led by the Politecnico di Milano and directed by R. Camagni and R. Capello. The authors wish to thank the 'stakeholders' of the project, namely the Diputaciò de Barcelona, the Départment de l'Hérault (Montpellier) and the Provincia di Torino for the constant stimulus, criticisms and contribution; and Sara Ferrara, member of the Coordination Unit of ESPON, who contributed in driving the complex consortium to a successful outcome. In the work presented here, different scenarios were further developed, the econometric model on NUTS-3 European regions was enriched with new variables and re-estimated, and the quantitative assumptions framing the simulation process were reformulated.

## 1.2  ALTERNATIVE PATHS FOR AFTER-CRISIS SCENARIOS

The first aim of the study is to build after-crisis scenarios. Its innovative reflection on this aspect starts from the idea that a trend scenario, understood in the conventional sense as an extrapolative, baseline scenario to which other alternative paths refer, does not seem meaningful in a context where numerous structural factors of strategic significance are changing profoundly.

A *reference scenario* has first to be built, and cannot refer to the past decades as the crisis has generated a clean break in the world development pillars: new driving components of global demand and trade, a new role of emerging economies, new geo-political power relations, and possibly new energy trends.

In fact, some macroeconomic and geo-political elements that characterized the pre-crisis decade are unlikely to be replicated in the coming years:

- the favourable terms of trade between advanced and emerging economies, particularly Brazil, Russia, India and China (the BRIC countries or BRICs), resulting from low production costs and slowly appreciating currencies of the latter countries, will no longer hold. Hence, the long-term support to real incomes in advanced countries, linked to low-cost imports, will decrease in parallel with the rise in wages and prices in the aforementioned countries and revaluation of their currencies, and also as a consequence of a possible decrease in monetary prices and wages in richer countries hard hit by the present crisis;
- developing countries will resist the previous strategy of financing Western public deficits, and particularly the US's rapidly increasing debt, for fear of likely currency devaluations, and turn to a wider financial (and perhaps monetary) integration within their own regions, namely South East Asia and South America;
- a sustained increase in world demand will no longer be based on debt expansion in private demand in advanced countries, as happened in the recent past, giving rise to systemic risks and monetary bubbles not only in real estate markets. Other sources of aggregate demand must be found, because the increase in imports by emerging, fast-growing economies will not be sufficient. In our opinion, a major role in this regard may be played by the development of a new production paradigm, that of the 'green economy': in fact, its spread could at the same time provide the necessary new source

of world demand – mainly in the form of new investments in renewable energies, energy-saving technologies and organizational methods – and new tools for boosting productivity in Western countries;

- some counter-effects of this beneficial trend may derive from increased bio-fuel production in agriculture (or the use of agricultural land for subsidized production of solar energy) at the expense of food production, exacerbating social difficulties and conflicts in poorer countries – the Mediterranean ones in particular;
- the reduction of growth rates in advanced countries, with the consequent reduction of international investments in lagging areas, may increase the push towards out-migrations from these areas, generating tensions of a purely political nature in southern European countries;
- relaunching globalization processes will be necessary, but on the conditions that the drawbacks which led to the crisis are avoided, and that better consideration is made of the need to preserve the know-how, competencies, knowledge and 'cognitive capital' that have developed over time in the production *filières* of European countries.

Once the reference scenario has been built on the above bases, other alternative, and even opposite, scenarios can be created on the basis of different assumptions on how economic actors perceive the structural changes brought about by the crisis: (a) a *proactive scenario* in which economic actors perceive changes and even anticipate them, through appropriate macroeconomic, industrial and legislative policies; and (b) an opposite *defensive scenario*, in which changes are not fully perceived by economic actors, and the general attitude favours the protection of existing structures, sectors, firms and jobs.

The initial study ended nearly a year ago (June 2010), and the book contains some reflections conducted at that time. An *ex post* judgement on our assumptions and interpretations shows that two years ago we were able, by and large, to anticipate certain structural breaks with an acceptable degree of precision, and to obtain some results unexpected at that time but which turned out to be correct. For example, the study was able to predict a slowdown in the national growth rate of Spain *vis-à-vis* the other European countries, something that was difficult to foresee at the beginning of 2009 given the good performance that Spain had achieved in the recent past and was still apparently achieving.

Moreover, as a consequence of the new geo-political games, the reference scenario suggested a possible relative shift from service to industrial activities in Europe brought about by some reduction in the terms of trade of European products with respect to those of the emerging countries, a phenomenon then beginning in some industrial sectors and some countries. The geo-political equilibria in the Mediterranean basin, influencing elements such as migrations and oil price, turned out to be another important element highlighted by the study.

The scenario methodology applied is characterized by being neither a pure forecasting methodology intended to obtain precise values of specific economic variables in the future, nor a pure foresight methodology yielding an image of the future based on radical breaks, on structural effects destroying past tendencies. Our approach can be defined as consisting in 'quantitative foresight': it involves in fact a scenario-building exercise whereby an image of the future is constructed on the assumption that some discontinuities will emerge in the main driving forces that influence and regulate the system. However, these discontinuities are translated into quantitative values and included in a model of structural relationships which, in traditional manner, links conditional (explanatory) variables and dependent variables, giving rise to a 'conditional' forecast. This methodology, which has been successfully applied in previous studies by the same authors (Capello et al., 2008, 2011), has the great advantage of being fully transparent in the qualitative–quantitative scenario assumptions but perfectly neutral concerning the single results, giving two forecasting models, the MASST and the MAN-3 models, the task of producing the trends and behavioural paths of regional GDP and population growth in each individual European region, under the above-mentioned alternative assumptions.

While this study contains an extension and upgrading of the original MASST model (Macroeconomic, Sectoral, Social and Territorial model), called MASST2, its entirely new feature is the MAN-3 (MASST at NUTS-3) model, which aims at providing GDP quantitative foresights at a more disaggregated territorial level than the MASST model. With use of the MAN-3 model, the quantitative foresights are developed at NUTS-3 level, the level of provinces and departments.

## 1.3 FROM GLOBAL TO LOCAL SCENARIOS: A COMPLEX METHODOLOGY

The second intention of the study is to build local scenarios in a global perspective. This requires the creation of a methodology able to merge the global driving forces that influence the world economy with the potentials of individual provinces in Europe. This has to be done in order to provide images of the future for regions and provinces in Europe perfectly consistent with the European global scenario assumptions.

The methodology applied guarantees such consistency through the following steps:

1.  identification of the individual driving forces of change that are likely to manifest themselves and the main fields on which they may impinge;
2.  construction of integrated qualitative scenarios on the basis of different, consistent assumptions on the most likely bifurcations in the driving forces and their interaction;
3.  insertion of these conditional elements into the MASST econometric model, estimated on the past causal relations and trends, through their likely impact on the future trends of the model's explanatory variables;
4.  identification by means of a simulation procedure at NUTS-2 of the most likely effects on European regions;
5.  inclusion of the conditional elements, together with the results of the previous forecast, in a second econometric model (MAN-3) interpreting the differential growth of each province with respect to its region – on the basis of its territorial assets; and
6.  final identification of the performance of provinces (NUTS-3) by means of a simulation procedure.

The scenario methodology used in this study has many and complex aspects. It consequently requires particular attention in all its steps.

### 1.3.1   Moving from Thematic to Integrated Scenarios

The complexity of this task resides first in moving beyond the single-dimensional logic of thematic scenarios towards the multidimensional logic of integrated scenarios. In the latter, the various single-dimensional trajectories must be related to each other, and cross-feedback effects must be taken into consideration. This requires a clear cause–effect logic which keeps assumptions carefully separate from effects, and hypotheses on the appearance of certain conditions distinct from results. Moreover, the assumptions on the driving forces should be as differentiated as possible, sometimes even opposite to each other, so as to yield differentiated images of the future on which to reflect.

The complexity of moving from thematic to integrated scenarios also involves the attempt to build alternative scenarios based on integrated assumptions about the general political, psychological and institutional setting and climate that may characterize the possible European reaction to the crisis and the subsequent development strategy. Two complex problems emerge in this process. The first relates to the already mentioned fact that a trend scenario, in the conventional sense of an extrapolative scenario, does not seem meaningful in a context where numerous factors of strategic significance are changing profoundly. A 'reference scenario' was already necessary to take into account the structural breaks brought about by the crisis. The second complex problem is the devising of a set of consistent assumptions that could characterize alternative but likely and politically relevant scenarios requiring in-depth exploration of their effects on the European economy, society and territory.

### 1.3.2 Moving from Qualitative to Quantitative Scenarios

The scenario methodology requires the translation of qualitative changes in the driving forces into quantitative levers of the two econometric models, one at NUTS-2 and one at NUTS-3.

The methodological complexity resides in the need to highlight, for each qualitative assumption, some levers of the model (exogenous variables), and to translate these assumptions into quantitative target values, due for the final forecasting year, on a transparent and a very strict logic. General consistency is required – and pursued – throughout the logical chain linking the general characteristics of each scenario to the potential trends of the main macroeconomic, technological and social variables, depicting in quantitative ways our main 'driving forces'. This applies to both the NUTS-2 and NUTS-3 simulation exercises.

### 1.3.3 Moving from NUTS-2 to NUTS-3 Scenarios

The methodology used to build scenarios at the intraregional level implies a new methodological step developed through the implementation of a simplified, simulation sub-model, the MAN-3 model. The sub-model is built so that the main trends and driving forces present in each scenario are considered and included in the forecasting process, together with the territorial specificities of the single regions of the three countries considered and which proved relevant to explanation of the relative performance of each province with respect to its region. The aspect of the MASST model not replicated at NUTS-3 is its comprehensive interregional interaction logic (with the international and interregional spillover effects) and the internal consistency of the macroeconomic forecasts.

The existence of these two models (MASST at NUTS-2 and MAN-3) yields advantages in the creation of the scenarios:

- MASST allows a more general and consistent scenario framework at NUTS-2, with strong interlinkage among all regions of Europe; and
- MAN-3 allows 'fine-tuning' of the conditional foresight with reference to the structural and territorial characteristics that explain the differential performance of each sub-region.

The MAN-3 sub-model is an econometric model which explains the differential GDP growth rate at NUTS-3 compared to the GDP growth rate at NUTS-2. In other words, the sub-model aims at identifying the reasons why a sub-regional area is able to grow more or less than its region. This interpretation is performed utilizing the concept of territorial capital and the quantitative measurement of its components.

Unlike MASST, the MAN-3 model is a purely 'distributive' model, in that it simply distributes regional growth among provinces of the same region using a typical top-down approach. The distributive nature of our model has a conceptual explanation. The endogenous capacity of local areas depends on the achievement of a critical mass of markets for final or intermediate goods, for input factors and for service activities. When NUTS-3 areas represent strategic core areas for the development of the region, and are able to explain through their dynamics most of the NUTS-2 growth patterns, the endogenous capacity for growth is already captured at NUTS-2 through the MASST model. In general, the achievement of a critical mass at local level is the result of close complementarity among economic activities in the different NUTS-3 sub-regions.

Conceptually speaking, the model identifies the reasons for a relatively higher performance of the province with respect to its region in the presence of territorial capital assets. These may be seen as the set of localized assets – natural, human, artificial, organizational, relational and cognitive – that constitute the competitive potential of a given territory (Camagni, 2009). The concept of territorial capital was launched explicitly in the early 2000s by the OECD (OECD, 2001) and re-launched by the EU Commission in its 'Guidelines to Structural Funds' in 2005:[2] agglomeration economies, equilibrated and polycentric urban structures, accessibility, skilled labour force, R&D and high-level education facilities, business networks and social capital, natural resources and cultural heritage, territorial diversity and territorial identities are indicated as the assets

---

[2] 'Each Region has a specific "territorial capital" that is distinct and generates a higher return for specific kinds of investments than for others. Territorial development policies should first and foremost help areas to develop their territorial capital' (CEC, 2005, p. 3).

and preconditions for regional growth that need to be properly identified, wisely protected and strengthened, intelligently utilized, continuously reinterpreted and reoriented.

In the forecasting exercise, interpreting the relative performance of a province on the basis of its local assets means highlighting which territorial elements will play a crucial role in the development scenarios; pointing out which sub-regions currently possess or may develop in the future these elements in order to act or react to the crisis better; and finally, letting the model draw a picture of the relative growth paths of the single sub-regions and define the likely interregional division of labour under different assumptions concerning the main driving forces.

## 1.4 THE APPLICATION OF THE SCENARIO RESULTS TO POLICY DESIGN

The interpretation of past trends, the construction of possible future scenarios, and the quantitative foresight of future regional development trends that are presented in this book suggest some clear policy recommendations that depart from traditional ones.

On the one hand, a wise macroeconomic policy should avoid the exacerbation of the crisis that may derive from excessively rapid and severe cuts in public expenditure, at the same time driving economies along a virtuous and credible path of debt reduction. An upsurge of private demand should be pursued through a wise mixture of measures to re-launch positive expectations and optimism among economic agents, prudent and well-targeted public incentives, the full perception of the cost advantage of a technological turn in energy use through energy-saving technologies and organizational methods, and bilateral and multilateral agreements on trade among the world regions.

On the other hand, generalized supply strategies favouring productivity increases and innovation should be pursued in harness with broad social pacts on employment levels and cautious wage increases.

But the main new strategy should be implemented at the territorial level through support for the bottom-up definition of viable, creative, and shared development and innovation paths by local communities on the basis of their own specificities, natural and artificial assets, excellence points, traditions and competencies: in short, by exploiting their 'territorial capital' and 'tapping the still untapped resources'. This support – simultaneously cultural, political, operational and financial – could come *in primis* from the European Union, driving in the same direction the development strategies pursued by national governments and regional/

local governments through new forms of inter-institutional synergies and governance methods.

Territory matters! It does so especially because it can provide the means with which to multiply the effectiveness of individual invest-ment decisions – in the sphere of infrastructure, industry, R&D, culture and tourism – if actions are taken within a spatially integrated and wise framework. Proposed in this regard is the concept of territo-rial 'platform' suggesting an endeavour to construct synergies among local actors: 'cognitive' platforms, integrating R&D, industries, high-level education; 'infrastructure platforms', multiplying access to new mobility tools and providing efficient interconnections; and 'identity platforms' integrating natural and cultural assets in prudent and enrich-ing exploitation.

Relationality and 'relational capital' are terms frequently utilized for various purposes: to emphasize the need for networking and cooperation among local actors, private and public; to support long-distance interac-tion, opening and collaboration; and to substitute simple financial incen-tives with agreements and partnerships, citizen participation and control in regional policy making. All these objectives indubitably require a broad reorientation of public policy styles in many regional contexts in the present Union.

## 1.5   STRUCTURE OF THE BOOK

The book is a monograph that starts from the first steps of the methodol-ogy, that is, identification of the driving forces. It then moves to the inte-grated scenarios, and simulates the quantitative foresights at NUTS-2 to be used as inputs to the new MAN-3 model in order to simulate foresights on the three Latin Arc countries at NUTS-3 level and for the Barcelona province. It concludes with the policy implications for both the Latin Arc province network and for the Barcelona province.

The chapters show a clear logical interconnection if read in sequence. However, efforts have been made to give each chapter its methodological autonomy and self-containment, together with evidence of its position in the full logical chain.

The book is divided into four parts (Figure 1.1). Part I is mainly devoted to the implementation of the after-crisis scenarios, starting from the thematic scenarios (Chapter 2) and the integrated scenarios (Chapter 3), and continuing with the regionalized quantitative foresight through application of the MASST model (Chapter 4). Part II presents the new innovative econometric model that allows the zooming of the regional

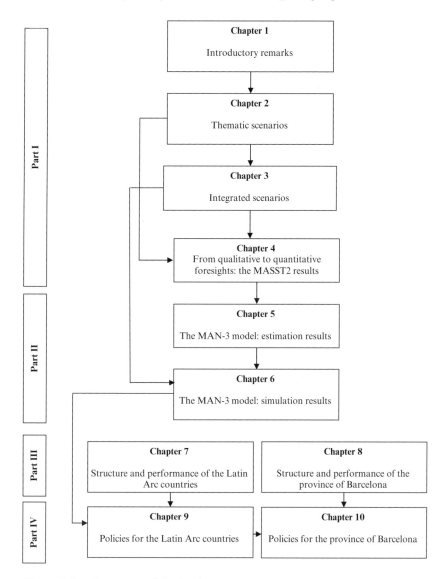

*Figure 1.1   Structure of the book*

scenarios into the NUTS-3 level. The new MAN-3 model is presented (Chapter 5) followed by the results of the simulations run for the three countries of the Latin Arc, namely Spain, France and Italy (Chapter 6). Part III is devoted to an in-depth analysis of the case study areas. First, the

Latin Arc countries and the Latin Arc province network are presented in Chapter 7, while Chapter 8 describes the structure and performance of the province of Barcelona. Part IV comprises the last two chapters, devoted to policy recommendations for the Latin Arc and the province of Barcelona, respectively.

# PART I


# Scenarios for European regions in a period of economic crisis

# 2. Driving forces of change and thematic scenarios for European regions

**Jacques Robert**

## 2.1 INTRODUCTION

Any serious foresight for regional development requires in-depth consideration of the main driving forces of change that are likely to be manifest and the main fields on which they may impinge. In the analysis reported here, the following fields were considered most likely to be profoundly affected by the huge transformations under way as a consequence of the 'global' economic crisis that hit the world, and the Western world in particular, in 2008–09:

- demography and migratory flows,
- economy and technological advances,
- energy,
- transport,
- urban systems and
- rural areas and rural development.

Many of these areas and the underlying transformation trends were already visible beforehand, but the crisis generated accelerations or sudden turnarounds in them: the propensity of advanced countries to give up manufacturing functions in favour of new emerging countries, keeping on-shore only 'advanced', 'control' and financial activities proved highly risky; the apparently endless possibilities to expand world demand for goods on the basis of debt creation and credit multipliers failed under the explosion of financial and real estate bubbles; the ageing of Western economies, whose rejuvenation was almost solely reliant on external in-migration, was likely to accelerate in the presence of the reduced wealth and attractiveness of advanced areas; and the possibility of a linear extrapolation into the future of relative growth trends, without considering feedback effects on international power relations, resource depletion, turnaround of technological leaderships, proved inconsistent.

Therefore, the main elements of a possible foresight were split into two parts: before (and during) the crisis and after the crisis, and the extent of the distance between the two was considered as indicative of the crucial jump in awareness, understanding and response capability to the crisis that is now necessary to counter its potentially disruptive effects on European territories.

More recent changes related to the emancipation of oppressed populations in North Africa and the Middle East were also considered, but less intensely, because their outcomes are still uncertain.

In this chapter, the present 'thematic' reflections on possible scenarios will be combined into three, alternative, 'integrated' scenarios emerging from the mutual interdependencies among the driving forces acting in each field.

## 2.2   EUROPEAN CHALLENGES BEFORE THE CRISIS

### 2.2.1   Demography and Migratory Flows

Demography has proved to be a real challenge for the development of Europe. While the population was abundant and exhibited sustained growth during the Fordist period, the long-lasting decline of fertility rates has generated modest population growth (average annual growth rate below 0.5 per cent since 2000) and progressive population ageing. Western Europe is not homogeneous in demographic terms, with some regions showing high population growth and others showing weak growth or even decline. Population change in European regions is largely determined by migration flows. The past decade has been characterized by sustained flows of migrants from Eastern to Western Europe, but also within Western Europe, and also between neighbouring countries.

Since 2000, fertility rates have increased slightly, but not enough to ensure the replacement of generations and to counterbalance population ageing.

The transformation of the demographic structure has significant impacts on the evolution of the working-age population. Since 2000, only 16 per cent of European regions experienced annual growth rates of their working-age populations higher than 1 per cent.

## 2.2.2 Economy

The European economy is now emerging from the most severe crisis of the post-war period. The recovery from the crisis is based not only on monetary policy operations to shore up the liquidity of financial institutions in response to the freezing of the interbank markets, but also on policies to mitigate the impact of the crisis on the economy. These have included massive fiscal stimulus, supplemented by labour and product market support targeted on hard-hit industries and workers. Moreover, new regulation and supervision frameworks have been demanded in order to reduce the likelihood of a similar crisis occurring in the future.

Yet, in spite of the substantial support and stimulus measures implemented since October 2008, the financial crisis is far from resolved. In 2009, economic activity fell by 3.6 per cent. However, this outcome conceals less-negative outcomes within the year, especially in the second half of 2009, due to improvements in private consumption, and investment in equipment and exports. The recovery trend was more accentuated in 2010, although with increasing performance disparities among European countries. This is partly explained by the stimulus measures adopted in line with the European Economy Recovery Plan (EERP). Particularly positive, albeit temporary, was the impact of the implementation of car-scrapping schemes in Spain and other member states, and of investment in equipment and exports. The policy response in Spain was twofold. On the one hand, expansionary fiscal measures to stimulate the economy were adopted in line with the EERP. On the other hand, a series of measures were implemented to support the restructuring of the financial sector, hard hit by the explosion of the real estate and construction bubble.

Austerity measures were massively introduced from 2010 onwards with the aim of limiting public debts and complying again with the convergence criteria (Greece, Spain, Portugal, the UK and Ireland in particular).

Major feedback effects of the crisis on public deficits, especially in countries characterized by large public debts and/or limited development capabilities, imposed severe restrictions on rescue policies and expansionary fiscal policies (Greece, Portugal, Spain and Italy). At the same time, doubts about the financial stability of some large financial institutes generated serious concerns about the possible transmission of shocks to the public sector, as in the case of Ireland, Spain, and in some respects also Germany. This general context is very different from the decade before 2008, when European average per capita income was more than three times higher than the world average, but it was only 70 per cent of the US level and lower than that of Japan. The process of convergence had come to an end at the beginning of the 1980s. Although productivity increased more dynamically in Europe, it was counteracted by weak employment performance and falling working hours. By and large, Europe had not sufficiently adopted the new economic paradigm based on new organizational forms, less vertically integrated firms, greater mobility both intra- and interfirm, greater flexibility of labour markets, a closer reliance on market finance and a higher demand for both R&D and higher education. Although the catching-up process of the economies of Central and Eastern Europe has been encouraging, with the 2004 and 2007 enlargements the EU inherited the largest levels of territorial inequality in its history. The Lisbon Strategy, adopted in 2000 to address the issue of European technological competitiveness, has been challenged by disappointing achievements. At the same time, the expansion of international trade and international investments has far outpaced the growth of output and income. The emerging economies (Brazil, Russia, India and China: BRICs) have played a major part in this process, using mainly their comparative advantages of lower labour costs and growing domestic markets.

### 2.2.3   Energy

The past 10 years have been characterized by strong fluctuations in the price of oil and by the price increases of other energy sources (natural gas, electricity). The strong fluctuations of the oil price between 2003 and 2009 were driven by both supply and demand variations: a marked increase in the oil price after 2003 (supply variations related to the Iraq war, demand variations, with increasing oil demand from emerging economies and role of OPEC – Organization of Petroleum-Producing Countries – and speculative traders); a large decrease in the oil price during the second half of 2008 caused by a sharp fall in demand related to the financial/economic crisis and the attenuation of speculation; and an increase in the oil price since mid-2009 caused by growing demand in emerging countries (mainly Asia), accentuated in 2011 by political turmoil in a number of Arab countries. The strongest price fluctuations concern crude oil, and they very closely reflect the relationship between supply and demand (no elasticity). The price evolution of other energy sources since 2003 shows an upward trend with smaller fluctuations, driven by the average change in the oil price. The liberalization of electricity markets in Europe has, to date, not resulted in a decrease of electricity prices. On the contrary, electricity producers increase domestic prices in the context of emerging competition so that they can invest to capture new markets abroad.

### 2.2.4  Transport

Even in a context of relatively modest economic growth rates, especially in the EU15, during the past 20 years Europe has seen a significant increase in traffic flows at all levels. Several factors have cumulatively contributed to this process: the progress of European integration, and especially East–West integration, the spatial segmentation of production processes in manufacturing activities, growing motorization, expanding urban sprawl and so on. Despite significant efforts, the development of transport infra-structure has not been sufficient to counterbalance congestion (roads, motorways, railways, airports). Wide disparities in accessibility remain, both in absolute and relative terms, which are progressively alleviated by the expansion of infrastructure networks (TEN-T) and by the spread of low-cost airlines. A major problem is the imbalance of transport modes in favour of road and air transport, which contrasts with the objective of sustainability. The significant increase in oil prices between 2003 and 2008 and from 2010 onwards had little effect on the volume of transport flows and on modal split.

### 2.2.5  Urban Systems

Between 1995 and 2004, all capital city regions in the EU, with the exception of Berlin and Dublin, increased or at least maintained their share of national GDP. The increase was particularly marked in Warsaw, Prague, Budapest, Sofia and Bucharest.

   The relative growth of capital city regions is strongly related to their attractiveness as locations for businesses, as well as for individuals. This tends to generate unbalanced territorial development within countries, unless there are other centres of economic activity, in particular other large cities or conurbations, or even networks of smaller cities and towns, to provide the same kind of attraction. The concentration of economic activity in capital cities brings benefits in the form, for example, of economies of scale or of agglomeration and the large size of markets. But it also involves costs in the form of congestion, poor air quality, and higher property prices. On average, the share of capital city regions in the national GDP increased by 9 per cent between 1995 and 2004, while the population increased by only 2 per cent. In only three countries in Europe do second-rank metropolitan areas seem effective in counterbalancing the economic power of the capital city: Spain (Barcelona); Italy (Milan); and Germany (multiple growth poles such as Munich, Frankfurt and Hamburg). In other countries, the capital city region tends to dominate; it does so even in Poland, despite relatively large concentrations of the population in Lodz, Kraków and Wroclaw. Only in Germany and Italy are there second-rank cities with GDP per head higher than in the capital (CEC, 2007).

In the context of accelerating globalization and of enterprise relocation to countries with low wages and booming markets (Asia in particular), medium-sized towns are generally more affected than metropolitan areas, both in Eastern and Western Europe.

On the other hand, the residential and tourist economy favours a number of attractive European regions with small and medium-sized cities. European integration is also an important factor in the development of urban systems at the intermediate scale across national boundaries.

European urban systems are also characterized by a significant increase in suburbanization. In 90 per cent of urban agglomerations, the population grew more in the suburbs than in the core city between 1996 and 2001. Population growth around second-tier cities with population loss in the centre is widely evident in Austria, Poland, Slovakia, Italy and Germany. Population growth in the suburbs is often accompanied by the suburbanization of economic activity. This is also the case of the capital cities in Central and Eastern Europe.

The spatial de-concentration of population and economic activities around agglomerations is accompanied by an overproportional expansion of the urbanized area. Over the past 20 years, the extent of built-up areas in many Western and Eastern European countries has increased by 20 per cent, but the population has increased by only 6 per cent. There is no apparent slowdown in these trends. The urban areas particularly at risk are located in the southern, eastern and central parts of Europe. The mix of forces behind urban sprawl includes both micro- and macroeconomic trends, such as the means of transport, the price of land, individual housing preferences, demographic trends, cultural traditions and constraints, the attractiveness of existing urban areas, and the application of land-use planning policies at both local and regional levels.

Social tensions and polarization have been growing in a large number of European cities over the past decade. In many cities, not only are unemployment rates high, but there are huge disparities in rates. Disparities are particularly large in France, Belgium and southern Italy (for example Marseilles and Catania).

Economic polarization takes place mainly in and around large cities, while demographic dispersal can be observed around an even larger number of cities, comprising also medium-sized towns. Various factors are contributing to this important trend: the deterioration of the quality of life in inner-city areas as well as in large, dense suburban housing estates; the growing concentration of low-income groups in cities, generating social segregation and feelings of insecurity; increased housing prices in cities; growing motorization, especially in the new member countries; and so on. Dispersal trends around cities are generally not spatially uniform and they favour corridors along main transport infrastructures.

## 2.2.6   Rural Areas and Rural Development

During the past decade, the differentiation of European rural areas has progressed further, increasing the contrast between accessible rural areas under urban influence (stabilization or increase of the population and the progress of counter-urbanization; stronger development of employment in secondary activities and private services) and the more remote and peripheral rural areas (strong population ageing; declining attractiveness for businesses and households; reduced provision of services; and, in various cases, vicious circles of deprivation). Intermediate rural areas are often characterized by the increasing importance of the 'new rural economy' (clusters, post-Fordism, learning regions and so on).[1]

The importance of agriculture in rural employment and in the outputs of rural regions is declining further. In Central and Eastern Europe, the share of agriculture in rural employment is still significant (above 20 per cent in numerous rural regions), but it is also rapidly declining. Agriculture is going through a slow transition process from 'productivism' to various types of para-productivist (competition on the basis of specialization, technology and strong links with agro-business) and peri-productivist (on- and off-farm diversification of activities and employment for farm household members) orientations. Agriculture is also affected by changes in consumption trends (growing importance of niche markets). The CAP (Common Agricultural Policy) reform, by introducing direct payments to farmers, as well as environmental and safety norms, has contributed to the evolution towards more sustainable forms of agriculture. However, liberalization measures, as for instance in the milk and dairy sector, are causing severe adjustment problems and significant tensions. Agricultural activities themselves show a growing contrast between large 'commercially oriented' holdings and smaller pluri-active and diversified units.

Numerous rural areas are benefiting from the increasing value placed by society upon the rural environment, culture and heritage, as well as

[1]   See ESPON Project EDORA (2010).

from the increasing ability of the urban population to access recreational amenities.

## 2.3   PROSPECTS AND CRITICAL FACTORS FOR THE NEXT 15 YEARS

### 2.3.1   Demography

The number of European regions whose populations will stagnate and then decline will grow. Population ageing will accelerate and dependency rates as well as mortality rates will increase in most regions. The increasing number of the 'oldest old' (aged 75 and over) will generate significant demand for health care. The size of the working-age population will further diminish in most regions. There are, however, regions in Europe where the demography is still dynamic, with large cohorts of young people. Increasingly, the winners will be the regions able to attract skilled manpower and/or well-off retirees. An open question is the amount of external in-migration towards Europe, especially in the context of the emancipation of oppressed populations (southern Mediterranean countries, the Middle East) and the related turmoil.

### 2.3.2   Economy

It is likely that wages will increase and technology will progress significantly in the emerging economies. Their traditional comparative advantage linked to low labour costs will progressively be replaced by a wider competitive advantage, challenging the European economies on world markets in segments of significantly higher added value.

Integration is likely to proceed more within the various world regions than between them. This may have significant consequences for the orientation of foreign direct investment (FDI). It is also not unlikely that Asian countries will create a common currency in order to protect their interests better. The future of the dollar as reserve currency is more in question than ever. Its further worldwide use in the trade of energy and raw materials is also uncertain. A weak dollar may, however, mean that significant production activities will be relocated into the dollar zone in order to gain better access to markets and also to export under better conditions. The accumulation of capital outside Europe (BRICs, energy-producing countries, sovereign funds) will facilitate the takeover of European businesses by non-European corporate groups looking for good investment opportunities, advanced technologies and short-term profits. This may endanger the long-term prosperity of increasing segments of the European economy. The probable increase of wages and related production costs in emerging economies (especially Asian countries) may induce inflation likely to spread throughout the world economy. The emergence of higher interest rates and mounting inflation is not improbable during the recovery from the economic crisis, and also for a longer period.

Being highly differentiated in territorial terms and widely affected by global trends, the European economy may follow rather different paths, each with its own territorial impacts. In this respect, the most strategic issue is how Europe will position itself at the global level after recovering from the economic crisis. Will the emerging economies (BRICs) become stronger competitors and induce Europe to adopt a defensive stance, or will Europe be pushed by the shock of the crisis and invest massively in new technologies in order to gain larger shares of external markets? Will the internal EU market of 500 million inhabitants be used more efficiently to let new forms of endogenous growth emerge, taking advantage of the complementarities existing among European regions? Will the political priority to curb climate change be utilized massively to change the energy paradigm and to generate economic growth through a 'Green New Deal'?

In addition to issues related to the global and macroeconomic context, intra-European issues are also relevant, such as the future extent of the catching-up process of Central and Eastern Europe. The engine behind this process has to date been largely the substantial amount of Western FDI in these countries. Will the flow of FDI continue with the same intensity and in the same direction after the recovery from the crisis, or will Western FDI be significantly redirected towards countries outside EU borders, further to the East and in the eastern and southern parts of the Mediterranean Basin? Will the countries of Central and Eastern Europe generate sufficient endogenous growth in order to compensate for a likely reduction of FDI?

To what extent will European regions become handicapped by the decline of the working-age population and by the scarcity of skilled manpower?

### 2.3.3 Energy

In the present context, energy prices are very closely related to the level of global economic growth. Despite strong price fluctuations in recent years and the fall at the beginning of the crisis, the general trend is upwards, as the troubles in the Middle East confirm. Recovery from the crisis and further development of the BRIC countries are likely to strengthen this trend. The energy sector is largely globalized because of the concentration of large fossil energy resources in a small number of countries. The external dependency of Europe in terms of energy supply will remain high in the next 15 years and will therefore be subject to the inelastic relation between global supply and demand. A possible depletion of oil resources in some large oilfields could generate a process of oil peaking (declining supply in a context of growing demand) which would result in extremely high energy prices.

The possible scarcity and depletion of uranium resources should not be underestimated in the context of the growing demand due to the construction of numerous nuclear power plants around the world. Coal will remain a significant energy source for the transition period between the old and the new energy paradigm. Thanks to new technologies ($CO_2$ capture), it will be possible to reduce considerably the air pollution generated by coal-fuelled power plants.

The development speed of renewable energy sources will depend on both the price evolution of conventional fossil energy sources and the political willingness to depart from carbon-related energy and to promote the new energy paradigm. The introduction of substantial carbon taxes would play a major part in this respect.

### 2.3.4   Transport

The main critical issues for the future in the transport sector are the elimination of congestion, the impact of transport on climate change, and the improvement of accessibility in less-favoured areas. The likely change of the energy paradigm in relation to climate issues and the possible scarcity of oil resources are major challenges for the transport sector. They will significantly affect transport costs and therefore locations (households, businesses) and mobility patterns. New transport technologies will emerge in the coming decade. The speed of their diffusion and generalization, however, is uncertain. If significant carbon taxes are introduced, the present modal split patterns will be affected to the benefit of more environmentally friendly transport modes. They will also have an impact on the mobility of people, favouring even more the development of information and communication technology (ICT) services as substitutes for physical mobility. Public transport networks and services are likely to be strengthened, both within urban regions and between them. High-speed train networks will continue their expansion, with new cross-border connections.

### 2.3.5 Cities and Urban Systems

Cities and urban systems will be confronted by a number of challenges during the coming decades. Some will be the results of trend continuation, others will be generated by the emergence of exogenous factors and new global priorities, especially those related to climate change.

Trend-related challenges concern the rebalancing of urban systems where capital cities and large metropolitan areas have largely captured growth in the past. This is a particular challenge for the countries of Central and Eastern Europe. Most challenges, however, are to be found at the level of metropolitan regions and urban entities. The continuation of urban sprawl in the surroundings of cities and growing social polarization with all related impacts (security, riots, social segregation, ethnic tensions and so on) within cities are growing concerns in numerous European towns.

Cities will in general be less affected by population ageing issues than the countryside, because of the presence of larger groups of young people. The demand for additional health-care services for the elderly will nevertheless increase.

Policies addressing climate change are likely to have significant impacts on cities, especially in the fields of transport systems and mobility, building and construction, urban planning, greening of the urban environment and so on. If energy prices increase substantially and/or carbon taxes are sufficiently high, changes towards more compact cities, especially with stronger concentrations of settlements around public transport network hubs, can be expected.

Municipal finances are particularly affected by the economic crisis and its impacts. Municipalities will find it increasingly difficult to meet the above-mentioned challenges with more limited resources. It is likely that local taxes will increase in a number of countries.

### 2.3.6 Rural Areas and Rural Development

As in the case of cities, the future challenges for rural areas will result partly from the continuation of trends and partly from factors of exogenous, mainly policy-related origin.

Numerous rural areas are likely to be affected by population ageing, and a growing number of them by population decline. Very much depends, however, on the situation of rural areas in relation to cities and metropolitan areas. This factor will play a growing role in the future with regard to the demographic and economic evolution of rural areas, as well as to the provision of services. This will contribute to stronger differentiation in the evolution of rural areas. The prospects for rural areas under metropolitan influence and for those which have potential for the residential and tourist economy are more encouraging than those of remote rural regions with declining populations, low accessibility and weak attractiveness. Agricultural activities will be significantly influenced by the further liberalization of the CAP and the growing importance of extra-European competition. The reformed CAP after 2013 will again condition a number of rural activities.

The strengthening of policies supporting the further development of renewable energy sources is of great importance for the future of numerous rural areas. Potentials exist in many rural regions, but they can be extensively exploited only if the profitability conditions improve. The introduction of carbon taxes is likely to increase the level of profitability of renewable energy sources, but it may constrain that of agriculture which also consumes significant amounts of oil-related energy.

## 2.4   CONCLUSIONS

The economic theme – encompassing the interlink between the financial and the 'real' aspects of the present crisis, the contradictions emerging at the global level which led to the sudden break of autumn 2008, the dramatic conditions of public policies acting under the opposite constraints imposed by the weakness of aggregate demand and necessary restrictions on sovereign debt – is bound to form the core of any foresight exercise concerning the future of the European territory. Major challenges will arise from this side, emphasizing the weaknesses and the risks already present in many other fields, such as demography and demographic ageing, energy prices and long-term energy shortages, environmental damage emerging especially from large urban areas, and increasing imbalances in territorial processes which are exhibiting the growing peripheralization of many rural and border areas.

While migratory flows will depend closely on the speed of economic readjustment by the European economies and the relaunching of core areas and large metropolitan areas and city-regions, technological development could furnish new opportunities for both growth – via territorial competitiveness – and environmental equilibria via more ecological ways of living, moving and producing.

# 3. Integrated scenarios for European regions

## Roberto Camagni, Roberta Capello and Jacques Robert

### 3.1 FROM THEMATIC TO INTEGRATED SCENARIOS

In the previous chapter thematic scenarios were presented with regard to the individual main driving forces of change. The more difficult task to accomplish now is implementation of truly integrated scenarios, considering all the possible feedback effects among the different driving forces and defining the main potential bifurcation points in the likely trajectory of the European territory.

The complexity of this task resides in two distinct aspects. The first is a methodological one. Building general, integrated scenarios means, on the one hand, moving beyond a single-dimensional logic similar to the one used in the previous chapter, where the effects of individual driving forces or the evolutions of specific fields were inspected (as in the case of a transport scenario, or a demographic scenario). The different trajectories must be related to each other, and cross-feedback effects must be underlined. On the other hand it requires assuming an 'if . . . then' logic, keeping assumptions carefully separate from effects, and hypotheses on the appearance of certain conditions distinct from results. In this sense, we do not construct 'good versus bad' scenarios, but rather 'conditional' scenarios based on assumptions concerning some crucial, difficult to forecast, general preconditions usually generating a discontinuity or a bifurcation in the trajectory of the system inspected. The difficulty consists precisely in maintaining a strong internal logic in the construction of these conditional scenarios, starting from a clear definition of assumptions and consistently deriving the results. Moreover, the assumptions on the driving forces should be as differentiated as possible, sometimes even opposite to each other, so as to yield differentiated images of the future on which to reflect.

The second, more operational, reason for the complexity of our task concerns the attempt to build alternative scenarios based on integrated assumptions about the general political, psychological and institutional setting and climate that may characterize the possible European reaction to the crisis and the subsequent development strategy. Two complex problems emerge in this process. The first relates to the fact that a trend scenario, in the conventional sense of an extrapolated scenario to which some alternative paths are referred, does not seem meaningful in a context where numerous factors of strategic significance are changing profoundly. What is called here a 'reference scenario' cannot refer to the past decades but must be built on the difficult interpretation of weak signals and scattered evidence, given that the crisis has led to a clean break, with new driving components of global demand and trade, the new role of emerging economies, new geo-political power relations, and possibly new energy trends.

The second complex problem is the devising of a set of consistent assumptions that could characterize alternative but likely and politically important scenarios requiring in-depth exploration of their effects on the European economy, society and territory.

In what follows, the reference scenario will be used as a benchmark for two additional ones. The main differences among the three scenarios consist in the different ways that economic and institutional actors perceive the structural changes brought about by the crisis. In the reference scenario, they will have a perception that structural changes will happen, but policies will not act effectively. This scenario will be compared to a second one, called the 'proactive scenario', in which economic actors will perceive changes and even anticipate them; and they will have a large capacity to proact by means of macroeconomic, industrial and legislative policies. The third scenario, the 'reactive' or 'defensive' one, will be based on the assumption that changes are not fully perceived by economic actors; the general attitude will be a defensive one to protect existing structures, sectors, firms and jobs; development assets will be more similar to those of the past.

In this chapter we present the three qualitative scenarios, namely reference, proactive and defensive. In the subsequent chapters the territorial effects of these scenarios, in terms of the growth potential of European regions and provinces, will be inspected through the use of two econometric models – working respectively on EU regions (NUTS-2) and on provinces (NUTS-3) of the Latin Arc countries, namely Spain, France and Italy – which will enable the definition and mapping of what we may call 'quantitative foresights'.

The role assigned to these quantitative exercises is twofold: first, to inspect the possibility of some counterintuitive result due to some unexpected cross-feedback among the different driving forces of change hypothesized in the scenarios; second, to fine-tune the potential effects of the scenario trends when they are compared with the specificities of EU territories and the huge structural differences among them.

Spatial effects of these scenarios are presented for the EU countries and also for the territories lying along the western Mediterranean Latin Arc, from Gibraltar to Sicily, most of which have joined the Latin Arc network through their province and department governments.

## 3.2 THE REFERENCE SCENARIO

As already stated above, the reference scenario is not to be considered a trend scenario in the conventional sense, because the simple extrapolation of past trends does not seem meaningful in a context where numerous factors of strategic significance are changing (globalization, energy paradigm, climate change, social orientation, recent economic crisis and so on).

Huge contradictions emerging in the recent past have largely been the cause of the present crisis: the debt-driven aggregate demand in advanced countries, highly sensitive to the conditions of the financial markets and widely responsible for the emergence and sudden explosion of the real estate and construction bubble; the financialization of Western economies, leading to an acceleration of change in the 'real' economy mainly on the basis of expectations, global comparison on returns, short-termism and speculation; and the bizarre evidence of new emerging countries such as Brazil, Russia, India and China (BRICs), which are relatively poor countries, not only supporting Western consumption (and real incomes) with a wide supply of low-price goods, but also supporting Western (and particularly the US) balances of payments with huge acquisitions of treasury and financial assets. All these elements, in fact, are due to change in the long run or have already changed.

The balance of the geo-political game will be different with respect to the past. Winning assets will be different. The dollar will no longer be the sole reference currency for international exchanges. A 'regionalized' globalization will probably take place, with the large 'triad' areas (Europe, America, East and South Asia) becoming more independent and more internally integrated, and also through new monetary agreements and unions.

The deflationary effect of Asia (mainly of China) on the world economy will be strongly attenuated and will progressively disappear. Inflation will increase as well as real interest rates. Purchasing power in Western countries, particularly of some groups (retirees, civil servants, low-income groups), will be particularly affected; the new generations will find it difficult to maintain their standard of living, eroding their heritage and property.

On the other hand, the BRICs will progressively enter in the medium- and high-technology game and will become sources of international demand, given the increase in internal per capita incomes. Growing oil and gas prices will favour investments in oil and gas exploration and discovery. The Arctic region will become strongly targeted in this respect. Regional tensions and possible conflicts cannot be excluded. The expansion of nuclear energy will be constrained by the progressive depletion of uranium resources. While European demography stagnates and the ageing process intensifies, a number of changes are likely to occur in the macroeconomic context. The regionalization of the global integration process will generate a geographical reorientation of foreign direct investment (FDI). The flow of external FDI into Europe will decrease, with the exception of those (sovereign funds and so on) aiming at taking over European businesses of a strategic nature (technology, brands and so on). Low labour cost investments will favour a ring of countries outside the EU (except Bulgaria and Romania), such as Ukraine, Moldova, Croatia, Serbia, Turkey and Egypt, generating major difficulties for the countries of Central and Eastern Europe, which are not yet at the 'cutting edge' of technological development and are progressively losing their comparative advantage of low labour costs. FDI will also favour new geographical areas, especially in Africa, Latin America and South East Asia, in order to develop local markets, create demand and exploit cheaper labour.

Hopefully, a lower real wage increase in Europe and the already mentioned 'regionalized' globalization will enable another structural break, namely a recovery of manufacturing activities, which will have to seek productivity gains in order to compete. If this trend comes about, disparities in the productivity of the main economic sectors are easily foreseeable, especially between advanced economic functions (financed by capital) and basic services (paid by incomes, including social transfers). The advent of a number of new technologies during the next 15 years will have significant impacts on the economy, especially in the fields of energy production and use, including the processing of bio-mass, nano-technologies, bio-technologies and transport systems.

The reindustrialization of Europe will not be space invariant: new manufacturing activities, benefiting from significant technological progress and from the related productivity growth typical of urban areas, will be attracted by well-developed regional locations. In addition to the main metropolitan regions, second-rank cities and metropolitan areas will also be beneficiaries, with the possible exception of a number of second-rank cities in Central and Eastern Europe which are handicapped by their low accessibility.

The most important effect of all these changes and contradictions, and the element on which new hopes for re-launching growth in advanced countries could be based, will be the emergence of a new paradigm: that of the 'green economy' driven by increasing energy prices and a growing concern about climate change. Its importance resides in its pervasiveness (hence the term 'paradigm'): it will enter almost all aspects of the economy. Many production sectors will be directly affected: energy of course, but also manufacturing, transport, building and construction, tourism, and even agriculture (production of bio-fuels and, most interesting, the emerging phenomenon of 'zero-km-agriculture' due to revitalize many peri-urban areas in a sustainable way).

The emergence of the green economy paradigm will constitute a large part of the new source of aggregate demand, desperately needed at the international level in order to replace debt-driven demand; but it will also provide new jobs in advanced but threatened countries and reduce dependency on fossil fuels. In brief, it may boost a revival of endogenous growth in Europe.

The perception of these structural changes, and consequently the speed of the international recovery, exists in the reference scenario, and changes will occur; but policies will not be implemented in an effective way. In the reference scenario, the profitability of renewable energy increases, but political support is insufficient to generate a radical change in the energy paradigm. The progress of renewable energy sources remains dispersed and fragmented, with low synergy effects. The economy benefits little from this process.

### 3.2.1 Territorial Aspects of the Reference Scenario

The catching-up process of the economies of Central and Eastern Europe continues, but at a significantly lower pace than before the economic crisis. It is also more differentiated among the countries concerned. Despite this macro-scale process, regional disparities are likely to increase within the EU at a lower level. The two-speed Europe is accentuated, with advanced economic functions concentrating more and more in metropolitan regions. New manufacturing activities also concentrate in well-developed regions. In addition to the main metropolitan regions, second-rank cities and metropolitan areas are also beneficiaries. Regions most affected by the crisis are mainly manufacturing ones with low or intermediate technologies and a relatively high intensity of manpower, both in Western and Eastern Europe.

Other regions affected by the crisis and where recovery proves difficult are those which, until the crisis, had booming activities in the building and construction sector. Lasting difficulties may also affect regions where economic growth before the crisis was largely based on financial speculation and related financial services or on specific fiscal niches. Numerous tourist regions have also been affected by the crisis, but tourism is highly volatile and the recovery of these regions depends upon the general level of the European economy. The evolution of rural areas will be contrasting and heterogeneous, with a number of rural regions being affected by the deregulation of the Common Agricultural Policy (CAP) and trade liberalization in the context of the World Trade Organization (WTO), others benefiting from the opportunities of bio-mass and renewable energy production.

The regions where demographic factors may act as a constraint on the regional labour markets are those where the economic recovery is substantial in a context of rapid population ageing. Immigration further concentrates in large cities, generating a low-cost housing market in their peripheries. It is also substantial in tourist areas and in areas attractive for retirees. In these regions, it fosters an increase of fertility rates.

### 3.2.2   Territorial Impacts for the Latin Arc

In the Latin Arc, three types of demographic structures prevail, with different development prospects. In the Catalan part, the young age of the population (sustained natural growth and positive migration balance) favours further population increase and limits the ageing process. In the French part, the population is, on average, older and is still growing, although to a lesser extent than in the Catalan part, mainly under the influence of migrations. In the Italian part, low fertility rates and a high share of the elderly induce a negative natural evolution, compensated in various areas, but not uniformly, by significant in-migration flows. The number of the 'oldest old' increases significantly, requiring a strong development of health-care services.

The Latin Arc has a rather heterogeneous economic structure, so developments will differ among regions. In general terms, metropolitan areas with advanced economic functions and technological poles are more favoured than cities with an economy depending upon intermediate or low technologies. After recovery, tourist functions progress moderately. The residential economy progresses more because of accelerating population ageing in Europe. Rural areas, especially the wine-producing regions, are affected, to a certain extent, by the deregulation of the CAP. A number of rural areas benefit from the production of renewable energy, but only a modest proportion of the available potential is exploited. Immigration is concentrated in metropolitan and tourist areas.

Cross-border accessibility benefits from the high-speed train connection between Catalonia and France (Barcelona–Perpignan) and between Rhône-Alpes and Piemonte (Lyon–Turin). Along the coast, however, the railway connection between Nice and Genoa is not significantly improved.

The considerable potential of the Mediterranean regions in the field of solar energy is not fully exploited, because of insufficient profitability and public support.

## 3.3   THE PROACTIVE SCENARIO

The proactive scenario is based on the assumption that the decisions adopted at the international level in order to curb the speed of climate change are used efficiently to generate significant economic growth throughout Europe. The implementation of the scenario requires the active involvement of economic actors and of civil society. A wide spectrum of sectors – manufacturing, energy, construction, agriculture, transport, R&D and advanced services – will benefit from the spread of the new 'green economy paradigm'; aggregate demand will benefit from new investment opportunities. The perception of changes brought about by the economic crisis is clear, and changes are even anticipated; the capacity of macroeconomic, industrial and legislative policies to proact is large.

This proactive scenario for Europe is part of a more global context in which the large emerging countries are pulling up the world economy while moving towards more technology-intensive activities. The international financial order is stabilized by the diversification of currency reserves, the dollar having lost its monopolistic position.

Economic growth is stronger and recovery more rapid than in the reference scenario. It is not limited to Europe, but includes the USA and Asia as well. The more-developed economies, and also the BRICs, invest in the less-developed countries, especially in Africa, Latin America and South East Asia, in order to develop local markets and to create demand, which is precisely the opposite of a protectionist attitude.

In Europe, the strategy consists of significantly increasing technological investments, boosting productivity but in a first stage generating higher unemployment rates. Only after a period of 5–7 years does employment begin to grow again. Higher skills and qualifications are required. The race for stronger tertiarization is attenuated by rapid development of the green economy which creates jobs in both R&D and manufacturing activities. Services move towards higher added-value segments. In the context of a more regional globalization, higher financial services are re-centred on Europe. Through higher competitiveness and stronger public support, European enterprises are less in danger of being taken over by non-European groups or sovereign funds.

Concretization of the green economy is far from easy. Numerous local authorities choose to take action with regard to climate change, but their resources are limited by the impacts of the economic crisis. Investments by small and medium-sized enterprises are constrained by difficulties in obtaining bank credit. The transition from carbon-related energy systems to a new energy paradigm more largely based on renewable energy sources is affected by the levels of investment necessary and by constraints of profitability. The international harmonization of policies is also a difficult issue which generates distortions.

The progressive emergence of new economic growth and the creation of significant numbers of new jobs after a few years, however, generate trust in the strategy related to the green economy, so that more and more businesses and households invest, with encouraging returns on investment. This leads to a mass effect which ensures sustained economic growth and strengthens social cohesion.

In the demographic sector, fertility rates revive, favoured by the positive economic evolution, but their impact remains a long-term one. The shortage of working-age population in a growing number of regions favours the immigration of skilled manpower.

### 3.3.1   Territorial Impacts of the Proactive Scenario

The territorial impacts of the proactive scenario change somewhat over time. During the first phase (5–7 years) growth is concentrated in metropolitan areas. In a second stage, production activities related to the green economy spread to second- and third-level cities, and also to regions of Central and Eastern Europe, as well as towards the more peripheral regions of Western Europe.

In the second stage, the scenario favours a higher degree of polycentricity in settlement systems than does the reference scenario.

In addition to economic aspects, the adoption of the green economy has important impacts on the morphology and organization of cities. More compact urban forms are developed in order to take advantage of the expansion of public transport networks. However, urban expansion is more contained and compact than in the reference scenario: the greening of cities and the further development of ICT limits motorized mobility for work and leisure purposes. Favourable economic development has a positive impact on social cohesion.

A significant number of rural areas benefit from the green economy. The positive economic climate favours the development of the residential and tourist economy which is beneficial to small and medium-sized cities as well as to rural areas with an attractive natural and cultural heritage.

### 3.3.2 Territorial Impacts on the Latin Arc

The scenario is favourable to the development of technology poles situated along the Latin Arc. The strengthening of R&D activities generates spin-off effects in the production sectors. In the context of the green economy, the development of solar energy booms along the Latin Arc, from R&D activities down to the general implementation of related technologies in rural areas and cities. An increasing share of electricity needs is met by the domestic production of solar and wind energy.

The implementation of the new cooperation activities with the countries of North Africa is possible because economic growth in Europe is significant. The metropolitan areas of the Latin Arc significantly benefit from such initiatives. The Latin Arc is subject to only moderate immigration because of stronger economic development in North Africa. A larger proportion of working-age immigrants are integrated into the regional labour markets of the Latin Arc, which are expanding.

The adoption of electric cars and the greater use of public transport contribute significantly to improving air quality in the compact and polluted Mediterranean cities. Traffic congestion is diminishing to a certain extent.

## 3.4 THE DEFENSIVE SCENARIO

The defensive scenario assumes a slow recovery from the crisis in the Western economies and Japan resulting from weak reactivity to the changing context and a lower perception of the new technological opportunities. Global demand remains modest. In the USA, domestic demand is much weaker than before the crisis because households give greater priority to savings than to consuming on credit. The BRICs maintain their comparative advantage in low-cost production. However, they also make progress in more technology-intensive sectors, and in greater competition with Europe. Few foreign investments are made in the less-developed countries of the world. Inflation is lower than in the reference scenario because of low wage policies in Asia with global deflationary impacts. Low interest rates feed new speculative bubbles, threatening the stability of the global economy. Maintenance of the dollar as reserve currency works in the same direction.

In this scenario, changes brought about by the crisis are not fully perceived by economic actors. The general attitude is a defensive one, protecting existing structures, sectors and firms; development assets are more similar to those of the past, and the risks of low development rates are higher.

Europe does not invent a new technological paradigm and fails significantly to modernize its productive activities. Because of insufficient public support and the modest mobilization of economic actors and civil society, the green economy cannot achieve a breakthrough. Service activities do not register a significant shift towards high-value services.

In the medium range (5–7 years) European exports are maintained, but they comprise a large share of products with modest added value. Employment is artificially protected in the medium range and the situation worsens thereafter because of insufficient competitiveness in the global context. Cost-competitive policies are maintained in Central and Eastern Europe in order to attract FDI. Their impact is limited, however. Exports slow down and unemployment increases. More European businesses are taken over by non-European groups. When the profits of such businesses decline because of the lack of investment in R&D and in productivity improvements, they are ignored by the new owners. The European population declines in the long run, as natural evolution is negative and immigration is strictly controlled.

### 3.4.1 Territorial Impacts of the Defensive Scenario

In the medium term, changes in the regional patterns are modest. However, the catching-up process of Central and Eastern Europe is significantly affected by the reduction in FDI after the crisis of 2008/09. The European settlement pattern is not significantly modified.

However, important territorial changes take place later on. The competitiveness of a number of activities in the agriculture, manufacturing industries and services sectors declines because of insufficient adjustments and productivity-related investment. The regions most affected are those with Fordist and neo-Fordist manufacturing activities. A significant number of rural regions are confronted with serious problems of decline in yields from agriculture and loss of jobs in small, no longer competitive manufacturing industries. The non-emergence of the green economy hinders the development of alternative activities in the production of renewable energy. Investments in this field remain dispersed and insufficiently profitable. The depressed economic situation does not favour the development of the residential and tourist economy in rural areas. The result is that out-migration from numerous rural regions intensifies, and not only in Central and Eastern Europe. Population ageing increases significantly and demographic decline affects numerous rural regions in the long run. The differentiation of rural areas accelerates.

New service and manufacturing activities concentrate mainly in and around metropolitan areas in order to minimize risks. There is insufficient economic potential and elasticity in the economy for a more polycentric development of settlement systems. Interregional migrations, which are more intense than in the reference scenario, favour large cities. Medium-sized and smaller cities which are not under metropolitan influence, and whose economies are strongly dependent on manufacturing activities, are particularly affected. The internal evolution of metropolitan regions raises concerns. Urban sprawl accelerates under the influence of the growth of population and activities and also of growing social tensions in the core cities. Social segregation, insecurity and criminality increase in inner-city areas and densely populated suburbs, where unemployment is significant. Traffic congestion increases and the share of non-polluting cars remains low.

### 3.4.2 Territorial Impacts on the Latin Arc

The lower level of public effort in the field of research and technological development does not enable the technology poles of the Latin Arc to generate spin-off effects and to contribute efficiently to the modernization of the regional economies. Manufacturing industries in the Latin Arc based on low and intermediate technologies are affected during the second phase, while the potential existing in the field of solar and other renewable energy sources is only modestly exploited. This is also detrimental for rural areas, which are confronted, in addition, to the decline in agricultural activities and to depopulation trends. The stagnating European economy handicaps the development of tourist functions and of the residential economy along the Latin Arc.

New activities concentrate mainly in metropolitan regions, adding to congestion and urban sprawl. External immigration is subject to stricter controls, but illegal immigration continues nevertheless, because of unfavourable economic conditions in North Africa and low progress in cooperation programmes with the southern Mediterranean countries. Second-level cities and medium-sized towns benefit much less from development. A number of them are affected by the decline of manufacturing activities.

## 3.5   CONCLUSIONS: EXPECTED MACROECONOMIC TRENDS

In this chapter, three after-crisis scenarios have been presented, starting from the contractions that have characterized the world economy in the recent past, and which are mostly responsible for the present crisis. The way in which the consequent structural changes are perceived and policies adjusted is assumed to be the main factor responsible for the differences among the three scenarios presented.

The emerging contradictions have been itemized as follows: (i) the demand generated by public (and private) debt in advanced countries, and unsustainable macroeconomic conditions in the long run; (ii) the constant shift of Western economies from manufacturing to service activities, with the relocation of industrial functions to emerging countries in order to exploit low wage conditions, with the risk of eroding core competences in industrial activities, and of losing control over the technological upgrading that accompanies industrial development; and (iii) emerging economies supporting Western consumption with low-price goods, sustaining Western real income thanks to the consequent low inflation rate, and financing the US trade deficit by buying US treasury bonds.

The consequences giving rise to structural breaks have been foreseen. First, the balance of geo-political games will be different. Not only GDP but also wages will increase, and technology will make significant progress in the emerging economies. Their comparative advantage may shift from labour-intensive to higher-value-intensive sectors, challenging the European economies on world markets in these sectors as well.

A 'regionalized' globalization would take place in this case, with significant structural changes for the European economy. A geographical reorientation of FDI would favour a ring of countries outside the EU (with the exception of Bulgaria and Romania), such as Ukraine, Moldova, Croatia, Serbia, Turkey and Egypt, generating major difficulties for the countries of Central and Eastern Europe.

But two major and more important structural breaks are foreseeable after the crisis: the possible recovery of manufacturing activities in Europe and the development of the green economy paradigm, both due to the creation of new jobs and new demand. The reference scenario registers the effects of the structural breaks leading to a permanent loss of wealth, with growth starting again from this eroded base (Figure 3.1a).

Against this background, the capacity (or incapacity) of the European economy to take advantage of the new global situation and its internal potentialities can be anticipated in the form of contrasting scenarios. In particular, two possible alternative scenarios have been built: on the one

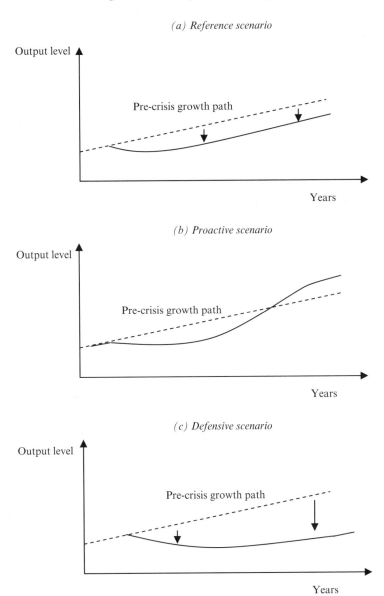

*Source:* Capello et al. (2011), elaborations on CEC (2010). With kind permission from Springer Science+Business Media: *Globalization and Regional Growth in Europe: Past Trends and Future Scenarios*, (2011), Roberta Capello, Ugo Fratesi and Laura Resmini (eds), Figure 11.6.

*Figure 3.1    Alternative growth paths out of the crisis: logical expectations*

hand, a proactive scenario in which these structural changes are perceived and even anticipated, and where the capacity to proact and react is large; this scenario would enable Europe to make a full return to an earlier growth path and raise its potential to go beyond pre-crisis output levels (Figure 3.1b); and on the other hand, a defensive scenario in which these changes are not perceived by economic actors, which remain anchored to the traditional development assets and miss many of the opportunities offered, thus risking low development patterns and a permanent loss in wealth (Figure 3.1c).

In aggregate terms, these expectations of ours are totally in line with those proposed by the European Commission in the Europe 2020 Report (CEC, 2010), giving them, in our opinion, a new rationale and justification.[1] Our expectations based on qualitative thinking require a quantitative validation, both in aggregate terms and at a territorially disaggregated level of analysis. This step is achieved by running simulations through the econometric MASST model, which is able to produce tendencies and behavioural paths of regional GDP at European NUTS-2 level under alternative assumptions. The next chapter is devoted to this exercise.

---

[1] In the Europe 2020 Report the three growth paths are labelled respectively, 'Sluggish recovery', 'sustainable recovery' and 'lost decade' (CEC, 2010, p. 7).

# 4. Quantitative foresights for European regions

**Roberta Capello and Ugo Fratesi**

## 4.1 QUANTITATIVE FORESIGHTS AT REGIONAL LEVEL

As mentioned in the previous chapters of this book, the world economic crisis has given rise to long-term breaks in the structural features of the economy stemming from recent emerging contradictions: demand based on debt in many advanced countries; growth of the financial sector in Western economies; Brazil, Russia, India and China (BRICs) supporting Western consumption with low-price goods; Western real income decreasing because of high inflation; and financing the US trade deficit (by buying US treasury bonds). As a consequence, at the end of the crisis, the balance of the geo-political game will be different, and winning assets will be different as well; the dollar may no longer be the sole reference currency for international exchanges; and a 'regionalized' globalization will take place. Needless to say, all these structural breaks will have strong effects on the possible future economic trajectories of regions in Europe.

This chapter presents advanced scenario-building and simulation exercises for the devising of anticipatory and far-sighted development strategies and regional policies in an era of structural breaks brought about by the economic downturn. It describes a reference scenario, built on the assumption that structural breaks take place, a proactive scenario reflecting the hypothesis that structural changes will be perceived and even anticipated, and a defensive scenario, in which changes will not be understood by economic actors.

The chapter is devoted to developing quantitative foresights on the three integrated scenarios presented in Chapter 3. In particular, a short summary of the methodological aspects of quantitative foresights is provided; and, especially, the empirical results obtained at aggregate and regional levels are described at length. The quantitative results will in general provide the same picture of the European territory in 2025 that we foresaw in qualitative terms, with a few exceptions that occur for good reasons.

The need for anticipatory and far-seeing economic visions has always induced economists to seek reliable methodologies with which to produce insights into what the future will look like. Among existing alternative methodological exercises, the distinction between forecasts and foresights is useful, and it helps specify the approach used in this book. In general, a forecast aims to obtain precise values of specific economic variables in the future, on the basis of extrapolations from a system of past socioeconomic relations. Exactly because they extrapolate from past tendencies, forecasts yield the best results in a short-term perspective. The aim of a forecasting exercise is, in general, to achieve a quantitative value in a certain year, paying little attention to the intermediate path, or to the feedback and adjustment processes by which the end value is determined.[1]

Foresight is a radically different exercise. It is mostly qualitative in nature, and its aim is to provide an image of the future based on radical breaks, in the form of structural effects which destroy past tendencies. A new techno-logical paradigm, new socio-cultural models and new political regimes are all examples of structural breaks in the elements regulating an economic system which give rise to completely new and radically different images of the future. A foresight is a possible, probable and sometimes desirable image of the future under the assumption that these events, or perhaps only one of them, will occur. In contrast to forecasts, foresights do not address the dynamic processes that will produce the final outcome; rather, they explore the general consistency of the final image by analysing all the adjust-ment processes that are likely to happen. In general, a foresight is built on an image of what the future will look like (explorative projections), but also of what the future should look like (desirable projections). Foresight provides insights into the future based on a structural and radical break with the past, and assuming in general a long-term perspective (usually decades).[2]

The logic of our methodology is not new. We have already applied it to other scenario exercises, the most recent of them aiming to capture the different effects of a long-term versus rapid recovery of countries from the economic crisis (Capello et al., 2011). The distinctive feature of this method-ology is that it is neither a pure forecast nor a pure foresight. Our approach can be defined as a *quantitative foresight* in that it is the result of three main steps (Figure 4.1). The first involves scenario building whereby an image of the future is constructed on the assumption that a discontinuity will emerge in the main elements or driving forces that influence and regulate the system. The second step is to insert these changes into a model of structural

[1]  On forecasting methodologies see, among others, Loomis and Cox (2000); Hawkins (2001); Hendry and Clements (2001).
[2]  On foresight methodologies see, among others, Miles and Keenan (2000); CEC (2004); UNIDO (2004).

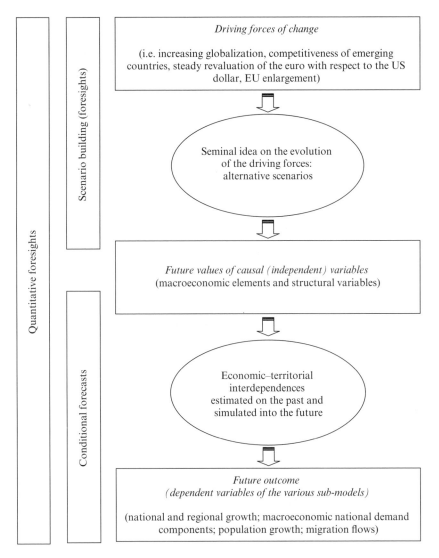

*Source:* Capello et al. (2008). With kind permission from Springer Science+Business Media: *Modelling Regional Scenarios for the Enlarged Europe: European Competitiveness and Global Strategies*, (2008), p. 1, R. Capello, R.P. Camagni, B. Chizzolini and U. Fratesi (eds), Figure 1.

*Figure 4.1   Logical steps of quantitative foresights*

relationships which, in traditional manner, links conditional (explanatory) variables and the dependent variables. For this step, our forecasting exercise relies on a macro-econometric regional growth model, called MASST2, an acronym recalling its structural features: a macroeconomic, social, sectoral, territorial model. To distinguish between the first (Capello, 2007; Capello et al., 2008; Capello and Fratesi, 2009) and the second, a more advanced version of the model (Capello et al., 2011) has been labelled MASST2.

The qualitative assumptions of the first-step procedure are translated into quantitative ones linking the expected driving forces to specific values of the model's independent causal variables. The third step involves a simulation procedure leading to a 'conditional' forecast of the dependent variables. Growth rates of GDP, industrial and service employment as well as their levels for each year up to 2025 are simulated.

Our approach is thus similar to a forecasting exercise because it is rooted in quantitative estimates of a system of relationships. However, it differs from typical forecasting exercises in that it inserts discontinuities into the driving forces of the system that allow for bifurcations in the system's dynamic trajectories. The structural relationships that hold together the economic system and its multiple linkages with the territorial system are assumed to remain stable in the transition from the past (estimation phase) to the future (simulation phase), but the combination of the main driving forces of changes in the transition gives rise to new, hypothetical but consistent scenarios.

In this sense, the approach is as neutral as possible *vis-à-vis* the results, leaving it to the MASST model to produce the tendencies and behavioural paths of regional GDP and population growth in each individual European region under alternative assumptions on the competitiveness strategies of different groups of countries. Before presenting the results, the main structural characteristics of the MASST model are now briefly described.

## 4.2   THE MASST MODEL

### 4.2.1   An Upgraded and Updated MASST Version: MASST2

The scenarios presented here are based on a more updated version of the MASST model – a combination of an econometric model of regional–national economic growth with a simulation algorithm – whose prime purpose is to forecast medium-term trends in economic growth and demography for the new Europe.[3] The 'territorial' element was rightly and sat-

---

[3]   A full presentation of the second version of the MASST model is available in Capello et al. (2011).

isfactorily taken into account in a first version of the model by means of a typology based on settlement structures in each region; NUTS-2 were divided among agglomerated, urban and rural regions, most of which proved to have an important role in explanation of regional dynamics. Found to be unsatisfactory in the first version of the model were the sectoral and the social dimensions: the former was represented by a simple variable, that is, the share of service activities present in the region; the latter by demographic elements. Both these solutions were dictated by data scarcity, and did not adequately capture the complexity of the cause–effect chain between a sectoral specialization or a social atmosphere and regional performance. Sectoral composition as well as local sectoral dynamics in the tradition of a shift-share analysis (Perloff, 1957; Perloff et al., 1960) should be taken into account and given a role in the explanation of regional growth. Theories of social and relational capital (Putnam, 1993; Camagni, 2002), highlighting the crucial role of non-material, intangible assets in explanation of regional dynamics, should be considered by a modern regional growth model, reinforcing its generative, bottom-up, capacity to explain regional performance. Moreover, in the first version of the model the effects of an international demand volatility were captured through simple changes in the constant of the export and import growth equations: a more precise indication of international demand changes has been required.

The second version of the MASST model has been built in order to overcome these limitations. The effort has proved worthwhile: the sectoral and social dimensions have been drastically reconsidered and now have a more solid role in explaining regional growth made possible by a recent collection of sectoral and social data comparable for all NUTS-2 regions of the European Union. These data enable exploration of the role performed by regional specialization/despecialization and by intangible assets such as trust in regional performances in the medium–long run (Capello et al., 2011).

These aims have been achieved without forgoing the most attractive aspect of MASST: its nature, in the words of Richardson (1969), as a 'distributive' and a 'generative' model at the same time, that is, as both a top-down and a bottom-up model. Indeed, the model allows for endogenous differentiated regional feedbacks of national policies and trends, and distributes them differently among regions, according to their capacity to capture national growth potentialities, following a distributive logic. In their turn, regional shocks, and regional feedbacks, propagate on regional GDP growth on the basis of structural elements explaining regional capacity to react to shocks. Regional shocks propagate to the national level through the sum of the regional GDP levels, giving the model a generative nature (Capello, 2007; Capello et al., 2008, 2011).

Other improvements on the first version of the model, besides full re-estimation over an extended time span (1995–2005), concern, at the national level, its capacity to take account of demand coming from different areas of the world.

MASST is an *economic* model, and therefore its outcome is mainly GDP, industrial and service employment growth rates and their spatial distribution.

The MASST model is a combination of two different and interactive parts: a pure macroeconomic regional growth model estimated on past growth; and a simulation algorithm for inspection of the future. Both parts will be thoroughly explained with regard to their conceptual and theoretical aspects.

### 4.2.2 The Econometric Model

In MASST, linkage between national factors and regional ones concerning growth is assured by the structure of the model, which interprets regional growth as resulting from a national growth component and a differential regional growth component:

$$\Delta Y_r = \Delta Y_N + s, r \in N, \tag{4.1}$$

where $\Delta Y_r$ and $\Delta Y_N$ denote the GDP growth rate, respectively, of the region and the nation, and $s$ represents the regional differential growth with respect to the nation.

Figure 4.2 presents the internal logic of the model, in which it is clear that the econometric model consists of two intertwined groups of equations, national and regional, giving both the regional and national components a role in local economic trajectories.

*National growth* depends on the dynamics of the macroeconomic national elements: private consumption growth, private investment growth, public expenditure growth and export and import growth. This part of the model is able to capture macroeconomic (national) effects on regional growth generated by interest rates and public expenditure policies, trends in inflation rates and wages. These policies and trends differ radically among European countries (especially between Eastern and Western ones).

In its turn, the *regional differential component* (the shift component, that is, the relative regional growth) depends on the competitiveness of the local system, which is based on the efficiency of local resources: the increase in the quality and quantity of production factors (such as human capital and population) in infrastructure endowment, in energy resources, as well as the sectoral and territorial structure of the regions and the interregional spatial linkages.

As a consequence of this double structure, MASST differs substantially

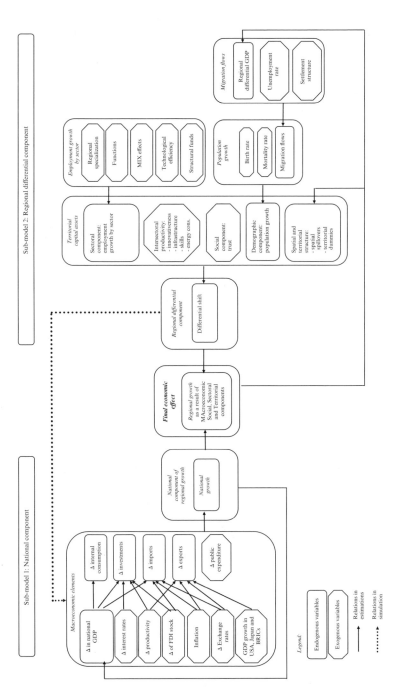

*Figure 4.2    The structure of the MASST2 model*

47

from existing regional growth econometric models. These conduct direct interpretations of absolute regional growth either by replicating national macroeconomic models or by using complex systems of equations for each region that are linked to both the national aggregate economy and the other regional economies through input–output technical coefficients determining intra- and interregional trade and output.

The first sub-model is a macroeconomic model, applied to each of the 27 European countries in our sample, which is very similar to the standard macro-econometic models used by national governments and central banks as programming and policy support tools. MASST differs from these macro-econometic models in that only goods and service markets are specified within it, while the monetary market, the labour market, and the public sector budget receive no endogenous treatment. The national sub-model of MASST is therefore a partial equilibrium model in which prices, wages, interest and exchange rates, and public spending are taken to be exogenous variables. If these characteristics of MASST can be regarded as shortcomings, they nevertheless allow a fairly simplified explanation of real growth as a function of policy tools (interest rates, exchange rate, government expenditure) or policy targets (inflation, unemployment) influenced by national or international macroeconomic trends.

The specification of the national sub-model consists of five equations. The first specifies the *private consumption growth rate* on a traditional Keynesian approach, depending directly on the growth of income (Table 4.1).

The *private investment growth rate* equation also has a traditional structure whereby the investment growth rate depends directly on the growth rate of output (as the accelerator model suggests), positively on interest rates,[4] negatively on a measure of the country's competitiveness (in our case, growth rate of unit labour costs, the inverse of productivity growth), and on the share of foreign direct investment (FDI) on domestic investments made in a country, given the domino effect that a flow of FDI may generate on domestic investment growth (Table 4.1).

The *import growth rate* equation is made positively dependent on changes in domestic demand, directly on the nominal exchange rate; on the internal inflation rate, and on the share of FDI flows on domestic investments (see Table 4.1).

---

[4] The nominal effective exchange rate (or, equivalently, the 'trade-weighted currency index') describes changes in the average value of a currency with reference to a given base period and a given group of reference countries. It is calculated by Eurostat as a weighted geometric average of the bilateral exchange rates against the currencies of competing countries. Given the way in which it is built, a rise in the index means *a strengthening of the currency (a re-valuation) and a loss of competitiveness*. The link between the effective exchange rate index and export growth is therefore expected to be negative.

*Table 4.1   Outline of the MASST2 sub-national groups of equations*

| Explanatory variables | Change in domestic output ($\Delta \% Y_N$) | Interest rates | Internal inflation | Nominal effective exchange rates index | Change in unit labour costs | Share of FDI flows on internal investments |
|---|---|---|---|---|---|---|
| **Estimated equations** | | | | | | |
| 1  Consumption growth rate ($\Delta \% C$) | + | | | | | |
| 2  Investment growth rate ($\Delta \% I$) | + | − | | | − | + |
| 3  Import growth rate ($\Delta \% M$) | + | | + | + | | + |
| 4  Export growth rate ($\Delta \% X$) | | | | − | − | |
| 5  (Pseudo) identity Output ($\Delta \% Y_N$) = $a_1 \Delta \% C + a_2 \Delta \% I + a_3 \Delta \% G + a_4 \Delta \% X - a_5 \Delta \% M$ | | | | | | |
| $\Delta \% G$ = Government expenditure growth rate | | | | | | |

Lastly, the *export growth rate* equation is expected to depend on the nominal exchange rate and on changes in the unit labour cost: for both explanatory variables, the relationship is expected to be negative (Table 4.1). The export growth rate equation also depends on changes in world demand, which are not explicitly mentioned as a control variable but are captured by the constant term of the equation.

The *government expenditure growth rate* is an exogenous independent variable of the model.

The national growth rate is determined by a *'pseudo' identity* equation derived from the national accounts identity: aggregate income plus imports ($Y + M$) must equal the sum of consumption, investments, public expenditures and exports, ($C + I + G + X$). By applying the total differential formula to the identity and by doing some simple algebraic manipulations we obtain:

$$Y = C + I + G + X - M \rightarrow \Delta Y = \frac{\partial Y}{\partial C} \Delta C + \frac{\partial Y}{\partial I} \Delta I + \frac{\partial Y}{\partial G} \Delta G$$
$$+ \frac{\partial Y}{\partial X} \Delta X - \frac{\partial Y}{\partial M} \Delta M$$

$$\frac{\Delta Y}{Y} = \frac{\partial Y}{\partial C} \frac{C}{Y} \frac{\Delta C}{C} + \frac{\partial Y}{\partial I} \frac{I}{Y} \frac{\Delta I}{I} + \frac{\partial Y}{\partial G} \frac{G}{Y} \frac{\Delta G}{G} + \frac{\partial Y}{\partial X} \frac{X}{Y} \frac{\Delta X}{X} - \frac{\partial Y}{\partial M} \frac{M}{Y} \frac{\Delta M}{M}$$

$$\frac{\Delta Y}{Y} = \eta_{YC} \frac{\Delta C}{C} + \eta_{YI} \frac{\Delta I}{I} + \eta_{YG} \frac{\Delta G}{G} + \eta_{YX} \frac{\Delta X}{X} - \eta_{YM} \frac{\Delta M}{M}. \tag{4.2}$$

*Table 4.2    Outline of the MASST2 sub-regional groups of equations*

---

1) Dependent variable: *regional differential shift*
   Independent
   variables:

   | Industrial sector dynamics | Average increase of industrial employment (lagged with respect to the dependent variable)* |
   | Service sector dynamics | Average increase of service employment (lagged with respect to the dependent variable)* |
   | Intersectoral productivity: | ● infrastructure endowment |
   | | ● share of self-employment |
   | | ● quality of human capital |
   | | ● population growth* |
   | | ● energy resources |
   | | ● human capital |
   | | ● rural vs. agglomerated vs. urban regions |
   | | ● MEGA regions |
   | | ● spatial spillovers* |
   | | ● EU funds (structural funds) |

2) Dependent variable: *average increase of industrial employment*
   Independent variable:
   Industrial specialization of the regions

3) Dependent variable: *average increase of tertiary employment*
   Independent variables:
   Past industrial structure Settlement structure of the region

4) Dependent variable: *population growth*
   Independent variables:

   | Birth rates | Death rates | Net in-migration* |

5) Dependent variable: *net immigration*
   Independent variables:

   | Regional differential growth | Unemployment rate | Regions' settlement structure |

---

*Note:*    Variables with * are endogenous variables in the model.

The regional part of the MASST model aims to explain relative regional growth with respect to national growth. It represents the novel feature with respect to the traditional regional econometric models of the 1970s and 1980s.

According to the logic of MASST, the higher/lower relative capacity of a region to grow depends on its structural elements: its productive structure, its relative position, its accessibility, its settlement structure, its degree of economic and social integration – all elements that identify a particular economic trajectory of a local economy which may differ from the national one. Table 4.2 shows the groups of equations that characterize the regional sub-model.

The first equation is the regional shift equation represented as a quasi-production function in a reduced form. It presents the factors thought to determine regional production capacity. These factors, which stem from both modern and traditional theories of regional growth, are the following:

- *industry and tertiary dynamics*, that is, the increase in employment growth in industry and in the tertiary sectors, capturing a sort of mix effect of the regional dynamics, demographic changes; and
- *an intersectoral productivity* stemming from structural features of the regions, such as infrastructure endowment, accessibility, share of self-employment, quantity and quality of human capital, availability of energy resources, and the settlement structure of regions, measuring the advantages stemming from the physical organization of the territory (agglomerated versus dispersed regions).

Not all the explanatory variables are exogenous to the model; three of them are endogenous and allow for cumulative processes, namely (Table 4.2):

- the *dynamics of industrial employment*, made dependent on the industrial specialization of the region;
- the *dynamics of tertiary employment*, made dependent on the industrial and settlement structure of the region;
- *demographic changes* (population growth rate) are dependent on birth and death rates and on in-migration;
- in its turn, *in-migration* is dependent on regional income differentials, unemployment rate, and on the different settlement structures of regions; and
- the part of regional growth dependent on the other regions' dynamics (*spatial spillovers*) is dependent on the regional growth of neighbouring regions in the previous year.

The way in which the recursive mechanism works over time in a forecasting model is of great importance for a full understanding of the logic lying behind the simulation procedure.

### 4.2.3 The Simulation Algorithm

In the case of the MASST model, the simulation algorithm has the specific role of creating a 'generative' process of regional growth. In other words, our intention was to create a model in which regional dynamics play an active part in explaining national growth and do not derive only from distributive mechanisms of allocation of national growth.

A conceptual distinction between *ex post* and *ex ante* national growth is useful, and it receives operational treatment in MASST. *Ex post* national growth rates cannot be anything other than the weighted sum of regional growth rates. If an *ex post*, competitive, approach to growth is chosen, the regional groups of equations only distribute national growth among the regions of the country. By contrast, if an *ex ante*, generative, approach is chosen, national growth can be obtained thanks to the performance of the single regions; in this case, regional growth plays an active role in defining national growth.

Our conceptual and operational approach follows the second definition: in MASST, the regional sub-model partly explains the national performance. Operationally, MASST treats *ex ante* and *ex post* growth rates as follows:

- *ex post* national (and regional) growth rates are obtained through the national sub-model and distributed to the regions through the results of the regional differential sub-model, rescaled in order to match the aggregate result (point C in Table 4.3); these results are considered to be the actual outcome of the model at time *t*; and
- *ex ante* regional growth rates are obtained when the regional differential growth is not rescaled; they are interpreted as 'potential' growth rates (point D) from which potential regional GDP levels are obtained. The sum of the increase in GDP levels determines the 'potential' national GDP growth rate in the following year (point $A_{t+1}$) through its influence on aggregate consumption, investment and imports.

Thanks to this simulation algorithm, MASST can definitely be interpreted as a 'generative' model: *ex ante* regional growth rates play an active role in defining national growth. *Ex post*, the national account identity is fulfilled.

The technical specifications of the model emerge from the structure just described. The model is first of all an *interactive national–regional model*. It combines top-down and bottom-up approaches so that an interdependent system of national and regional effects is built (Figure 4.3). This structure enables account to be taken of vertical and horizontal feedbacks between the regional and the national economy. In fact, thanks to its structure, the MASST model is able to register the effects of a shock at the national level (whether a change in macroeconomic trends or a policy choice) on both the

*Table 4.3    Logic of the simulation procedure*

| Forecasts | Year *t*\* | Year *t*+1 (and thereafter) |
|---|---|---|
| Estimated national growth | (A$_t$) Calculation of actual *national growth* with the national sub-model (output of MASST at time *t*) | (A$_{t+1}$) Calculation of actual *national growth* with the national model, as a function of lagged potential growth (output of MASST at *t*+1) |
| | (B$_t$) Calculation of *regional differential shift* with the regional sub-model | (B$_{t+1}$) Calculation of *regional differential shift* with the regional model |
| Estimated regional growth | (C$_t$) Actual regional growth is calculated as the *sum of A and B*, where B is rescaled to have 0 mean within each country (output of MASST at time *t*) | (C$_{t+1}$) Regional growth is calculated as the *sum of A and B*, where B is rescaled to have 0 mean within each country (output of MASST at *t*+1) |
| | (D$_t$) Potential regional growth is equal to the *sum of A and B* (non-rescaled) Potential national growth is equal to the increase in the sum of potential regional income levels in D$_t$ | (D$_{t+1}$) Potential regional growth is equal to the *sum of A and B* (non-rescaled) Potential national growth is equal to the increase in the sum of potential regional income levels in D$_{t+1}$ |

*Note:*  \* The last year for which official statistics were available at the beginning of the estimations was 2002.

*Source:*  Capello et al. (2008). With kind permission from Springer Science+Business Media: *Modelling Regional Scenarios for the Enlarged Europe: European Competitiveness and Global Strategies*, (2008), p. 95, R. Capello, R.P. Camagni, B. Chizzolini and U. Fratesi (eds), Table 5.4.

national and regional growth rates; moreover, it is able to interpret the effects of a shock at regional level on both the national and regional performances.

The model allows for endogenous differentiated regional feedbacks from national policies and trends; it captures the vertical feedbacks of a national policy on regional growth and distributes them differently among regions according to their capacity to capture national growth potentialities (regional growth spillovers, settlement structure). Table 4.4 shows

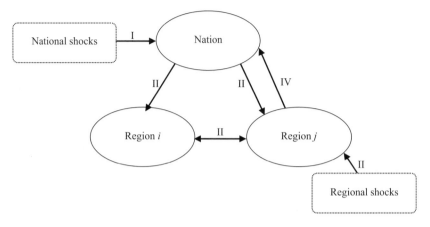

*Note:* The numbers next to the arrows refer to Table 4.4, where the mechanisms of national–regional linkages are explained.

*Source:* Capello et al. (2008). With kind permission from Springer Science+Business Media: *Modelling Regional Scenarios for the Enlarged Europe: European Competitiveness and Global Strategies*, (2008), p. 96, R. Capello, R.P. Camagni, B. Chizzolini and U. Fratesi (eds), Figure 5.2.

*Figure 4.3    National–regional linkages in MASST*

*Table 4.4    Measurement methods of interactive national–regional linkages*

| Effects<br><br>Shocks | National | Regional |
|---|---|---|
| National | I<br>National effects measured through dynamic national income growth present in the estimation procedure | II<br>Regional effects measured through the national component in regional growth compounded by regional growth spillovers and territorial dummies present in the estimation procedure |
| Regional | IV<br>National effects measured through the national income growth obtained as an increase in regional income levels in the simulation procedure | III<br>Regional effects measured through the presence of regional control variables and spillovers in the estimation procedure |

*Source:* Capello et al. (2008). With kind permission from Springer Science+Business Media: *Modelling Regional Scenarios for the Enlarged Europe: European Competitiveness and Global Strategies*, (2008), p. 97, R. Capello, R.P. Camagni, B. Chizzolini and U. Fratesi (eds), Table 5.5.

how these linkages take place. National shocks are registered on national GDP growth rates through the national GDP growth present in the consumption and import growth equations. National shocks propagate to the regional level since regional GDP growth is obtained as the sum of the national GDP growth and the regional differential GDP growth. The latter is distributed differently among regions via spillover effects and territorial dummies.

Regional shocks, and regional feedbacks, propagate on regional GDP growth thanks to the shift equation: regional shocks differ among regions because of spillovers, dummy variables and different levels of the control variables. Regional shocks propagate to the national level through the sum of the regional GDP levels which defines the annual national GDP growth. This feedback is the only one that takes place in the simulation and not in the estimation procedure.

Moreover, the MASST model is an *integrated model*. Its structure allocates specific places to both socioeconomic and spatial (horizontal) feedbacks among regional economies. While the former are captured by the socioeconomic conditions generating interregional migration flows, the latter are measured by spatial spillover effects, the growth rate of a region being also dependent on the growth rate of neighbouring regions.

MASST does not confine its explanation of regional growth to economic material resources alone. Two elements of a different nature are important in determining regional growth in the model: relational and spatial elements. In MASST, regional growth is in fact also conceived as a relational and a spatial process: demographic (population growth and migration flows) and territorial tendencies perform an important role in explaining regional growth differentials. In the case of relational elements, data unavailability admittedly hampers full empirical analysis of this dimension, which at present is replaced by socio-demographic phenomena such as migration. It is nevertheless important theoretically to stress its importance and to suggest future data collections in this area at regional level. The spatial and territorial dimensions help explain regional growth in two ways. First, the model directly captures proximity effects through the measurement of spatial spillovers; moreover, with the introduction of variables interpreting the territorial (agglomerated, urbanized, rural) structure, the model indirectly measures the agglomeration economy (diseconomy) effects that influence growth (decline) in a cumulative way.

Another important feature of the model is that it is an endogenous, local competitiveness-driven model to explain regional growth, as we expected it to be. Regional growth is explained by local factors, and interregional competitiveness stems from specific locational advantages and resource endowment.

MASST is a macroeconomic (multinational) model. Short-term (macroeconomic) effects are dealt with at the national level, and their feedbacks on national and regional economies are taken into consideration in explaining local dynamic patterns. MASST is a dynamic model. The outcome of one period of time at both national and regional levels enters the definition of the output of the following period, in a cumulative and self-reinforcing development pattern. As mentioned above, MASST is a *generative* regional growth model in which regional performance influences national growth patterns. It is this feature that distinguishes the model from the ones present in the literature. Given the above characteristics, the model is a *multi-layer, policy impact assessment model.* The structure of the model, in fact, allows measurement of the impact of national (and supranational) policy instruments on both regional and national growth, and the impact of regional policies on national and regional growth.

## 4.3   QUANTITATIVE SCENARIO ASSUMPTIONS

Quantitative scenarios come from the translation of the integrated scenarios of Chapter 3 into a quantitative model which is able to represent the results at NUTS-2 level of the European patterns of growth in the scenarios.

NUTS-2 foresights for the whole of Europe are necessary since they allow prediction of economic growth rates under different scenarios for the various regions, taking into account:

- the macroeconomic conditions, which affect all Europe and the various countries, so that the growth rate of any region is not independent from that of its respective country and that of Europe; and
- the effects of regional interactions, since no region is a world apart but its growth rate also depends on its interactions with neighbouring regions.

In order to produce foresights with the MASST2 model, the qualitative assumptions of the integrated scenarios need to be translated into quantitative assumptions, that is, hypotheses on the actual value that some exogenous variables will take at the end of the simulation period (that is, in 2025). These are called the 'quantitative levers' of the model, and can be observed in Table 4.5, which reports the correspondence between the quantitative assumptions and the levers used in the model. For example, the attenuation of the deflationary effect of Asia on the world economies

*Table 4.5   The levers of the MASST2 model in the three scenarios*

(a) *Reference scenario*

| Scenario assumptions | MASST assumptions (with respect to the past) |
| --- | --- |
| Reduction of the amount of external FDI into Europe | Reduction in the share of FDI on GFCF[1] |
| Loss of importance by the US dollar as reserve currency | Revaluation of euro |
| Deflationary effect of Asia on world economies attenuated | Higher inflation rates with respect to the past |
| Recovery of some manufacturing activities in Europe, especially open ones | Increase in growth rates of open sectors and decrease in the others |
| A number of new technologies will develop: nano-tech, bio-tech, transport technologies, new materials | Increase in growth rates of open sectors and decrease in the others |
| Ageing and immigration in largest cities | Increase in death rates and decrease in birth rates, stronger in non-agglomerated regions |
| Rising interest rates | Rising interest rates |
| Limited trade increase | Lower constant of import and exports equations |
| BRICs progressively enter the medium- and high-technology game | High growth rate of BRICs |
| Increase in oil prices due to oil demand increase: new investments in exploration and discovery | Increase in energy prices |

(b) *Proactive scenario*

| Scenario assumptions | MASST assumptions (with respect to reference scenario) |
| --- | --- |
| BRIC countries also moving towards more technology-intensive activities with better-paid jobs; disappearance of deflationary effect of Asia on world economies | Higher increase in BRIC growth rates |
| Recovery also in USA and Japan | Higher growth in USA and Japan |
| Loss of importance by the US dollar as reserve currency; euro revaluation | Euro revaluation |

*Table 4.5*   (continued)

| Scenario assumptions | MASST assumptions (with respect to reference scenario) |
| --- | --- |
| A more stable international financial order emerges | Only slightly higher inflation, despite high growth |
| Higher technological investments and productivity in Europe | Lower unit labour costs |
| Higher skills and qualifications required | Higher HRST[2], especially in strong regions |
| Increase in oil prices due to oil demand increase, partially counterbalanced by the development of the green economy | Lower increase in energy prices |
| Advanced economies moving towards technology-oriented activities, resolutely implementing the green economy | Lower increase in energy consumption |
| Technological investments boost productivity; unemployment rates increase further in a first phase (5 to 7 years) and decrease significantly afterwards | Higher unemployment rates, especially in weakest areas |
| Increase of service activities attenuated thanks to a rapid development of the green economy | Increased growth rate of open sectors and increase in advanced service sectors |
| Investments from Europe and BRICs in poor countries (such as Africa) will increase in order to create local markets
Non-European FDI will slow down, but BRICs and sovereign fund investments will endanger the EU's competitiveness | Lower FDI in eastern regions |
| Impact of demographic change on (skilled) manpower shortage | Higher birth rates and lower mortality rates especially in weaker areas |

(c) *Defensive scenario*

| Scenario assumptions | MASST assumptions (with respect to reference scenario) |
| --- | --- |
| Deflationary effect of Asia persists: inflation rate is lower | Lower inflation rate |

*Table 4.5*   (continued)

| Scenario assumptions | MASST assumptions (with respect to reference scenario) |
|---|---|
| The euro does not become a reliable reserve currency | Lower revaluation of euro |
| More European businesses are taken over by non-European groups, which means in a first instance more inward capital flows. These, however, are for short-term profits and for appropriation of technology | Higher FDI in eastern regions |
| In the US internal demand remains low, because households give higher priority to savings than to consumption | Lower growth rate of USA and Japan |
| BRICs maintain their comparative advantage in low-cost production; however, they progress also in more technology-intensive sectors, competing more intensively with Europe | Lower growth rate of BRICs |
| The service sector is less qualified than in the reference scenario. Low-profile tertiary activities, such as call centres, dominate | Decreased growth rate of open sectors and increase in base tertiary sectors |
| Loss of competitiveness by the European system in the long run | Lower increase in human resource in science and technology |
| Less increase in oil prices; the increase is partially due to the use of traditional energy technologies | Lower increase in energy prices |
| The green economy cannot achieve a real breakthrough | Higher energy consumption |
| While employment remains relatively protected during the first phase (5 to 7 years), the situation worsens afterwards | Lower unemployment rates, especially in weaker areas |

*Notes:*
1.   GFCF = gross fixed capital formation.
2.   HRST = human resources in science and technology.

is reflected in different assumptions concerning the value of inflation within the EU, with inflation assumed higher in the proactive scenario, where the BRIC countries move towards technology-intensive activities and the deflationary effect disappears, and lower in the defensive scenario where the deflationary effect is strong. Another example is the qualitative assumption of the dollar as the reference currency. If the dollar is no longer the reference currency (as is the case in the proactive scenario), the exchange rates of the European currencies, and the euro in particular, are revalued.

The same mechanism also works at the regional level, with in addition the possibility of introducing differentiations by type of region. For example, the assumption of population ageing is translated into a quantitative assumption in the MASST through an increase in the mortality rate and a decrease in the fertility rate.

Finally, some assumptions act at the sectoral level, so that the assumptions of the defensive scenario that low-level activities dominate is reflected by a relatively higher growth rate of low-level service activities and a relatively lower growth rate of open sectors.

The translation of the qualitative assumptions presented earlier into the quantitative levers of the model is presented in Table 4.6. The quantitative values are presented in Figures 4A2.1 and 4A2.2.

In this way, the quantitative scenarios presented here are fully consistent with the qualitative scenarios described earlier: the quantitative exercise makes it possible to test whether the logic expectations presented in the qualitative scenarios are confirmed by a strictly logical and consistent macroeconomic model.

## 4.4    AGGREGATE PERFORMANCE

Figure 4.4 reports the aggregate per capita GDP level from 2010 to 2025 forecast by the MASST2 model in the three scenarios presented in Chapter 3, compared to a baseline scenario which extrapolates the recent pre-crisis trends without considering the structural breakdown generated by the crisis itself.

In line with our conceptual expectations, the reference scenario shows a lower GDP per capita trend with respect to a pre-crisis scenario (Figure 4.4a). When structural breaks due to the crisis are perceived, and even anticipated by policy makers, as assumed in the proactive scenario, the capacity of the economic system to grow is much higher than in a pre-crisis scenario (Figure 4.4b). The defensive scenario, in which economic actors and governments do not adjust their behaviour to these structural changes,

*Table 4.6 The assumptions of the three scenarios for the MASST2 model*

| Driving forces | Reference scenario | A proactive scenario | A defensive scenario |
|---|---|---|---|
| 1. A regionalized global economy | • Deflationary effect of Asia on world economies attenuated<br>• Rising interest rates<br>• Recovery of some manufacturing activities in Europe, especially open ones<br>• Limited trade increase<br>• BRICs enter progressively in the medium- and high-technology game | • BRIC countries also moving towards more technology-intensive activities with better-paid jobs; deflationary effect of Asia on world economies disappears<br>• The dollar is no longer the sole reserve currency; it devaluates with respect to the euro<br>• A more stable international financial order emerges<br>• Higher technological investments and productivity in Europe<br>• Race towards stronger service sectors attenuated thanks to a rapid development of the green economy<br>• Investments from Europe and BRICs in poor countries (such as Africa) will increase in order to create local markets | • Deflationary effect of Asia persists: inflation rate is lower<br>• The dollar remains the sole reserve currency. It revalues with respect to the euro<br>• More European businesses are taken over by non-European groups, which means in a first instance more inward capital flows. These, however, are for short-term profits and for appropriation of technology<br>• Internal demand in the US remains low, because households give higher priority to savings than to consumption<br>• BRICs maintain their comparative advantage in low-cost production; however, they progress also in more technology-intensive sectors, competing more intensively with Europe |

Table 4.6 (continued)

| Driving forces | Reference scenario | A proactive scenario | A defensive scenario |
|---|---|---|---|
| | | • Non-European FDI will slow down, but BRICs and sovereign fund investments will endanger competitiveness of EU <br> • Impact of demographic change on (skilled) manpower shortage | • The service sector is less qualified than in the reference scenario. Low-profile tertiary activities such as call centres, dominate <br> • Loss of competitiveness by the European system in the long run |
| 2. Rise of energy price | • Increase in oil prices due to oil demand increase: new investments in exploration and discovery <br> • A number of new technologies will develop: nano-tech, bio-tech, transport technologies, new materials | • Increase in oil prices due to oil demand increase, partially counterbalanced by the development of the green economy | • Less increase in oil prices; the increase is partially due to the use of traditional energy technologies |
| 3. A new paradigm: 'the green economy' | • Many sectors affected: manufacturing, energy, transport, building and construction, tourism, agriculture (zero-km) | • Advanced economies moving towards technology-oriented activities, resolutely implementing the green economy | • The green economy cannot achieve a real breakthrough |

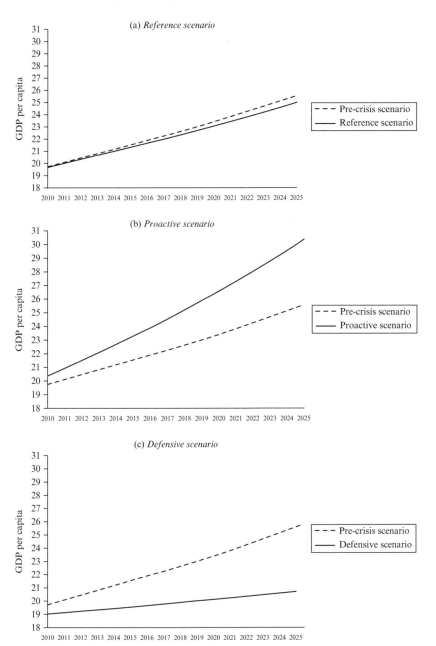

*Figure 4.4    Alternative growth paths out of the crisis: a quantitative analysis*

*Table 4.7    Average annual growth rates of GDP and employment in the three scenarios, 2005–2025*

| | Reference scenario | Proactive scenario (A) | Defensive scenario (B) | Difference between A and reference | Difference between B and reference |
|---|---|---|---|---|---|
| *GDP per capita growth rates* | | | | | |
| EU27 | 2.06 | 3.06 | 1.09 | 1.00 | −0.98 |
| Old 15 | 2.05 | 3.05 | 1.08 | 1.00 | −0.97 |
| New 12 | 2.29 | 3.38 | 1.20 | 1.09 | −1.09 |
| Latin Arc countries | 1.96 | 2.94 | 0.98 | 0.98 | −0.98 |
| Spain | 2.06 | 3.02 | 1.02 | 0.96 | −1.04 |
| France | 1.99 | 2.97 | 1.02 | 0.97 | −0.97 |
| Italy | 1.83 | 2.83 | 0.89 | 1.00 | −0.95 |
| *Total employment* | | | | | |
| EU27 | 0.64 | 1.30 | 0.61 | 0.67 | −0.02 |
| Old15 | 0.57 | 1.24 | 0.57 | 0.67 | −0.01 |
| New12 | 0.93 | 1.61 | 0.85 | 0.68 | −0.08 |
| Latin Arc countries | 0.80 | 1.47 | 0.83 | 0.66 | 0.03 |
| Spain | 1.17 | 1.88 | 1.26 | 0.71 | 0.09 |
| France | 0.45 | 1.09 | 0.42 | 0.64 | −0.03 |
| Italy | 0.86 | 1.50 | 0.88 | 0.64 | 0.02 |
| *Manufacturing employment* | | | | | |
| EU27 | −0.79 | −0.57 | −0.82 | 0.23 | −0.03 |
| Old15 | −0.93 | −0.72 | −0.97 | 0.22 | −0.04 |
| New12 | −0.34 | −0.09 | −0.32 | 0.26 | 0.02 |
| Latin Arc countries | −0.56 | −0.34 | −0.56 | 0.22 | 0.00 |
| Spain | −0.27 | −0.09 | −0.27 | 0.18 | 0.01 |
| France | −1.09 | −0.87 | −1.10 | 0.21 | −0.01 |
| Italy | −0.41 | −0.16 | −0.40 | 0.25 | 0.01 |
| *Service employment* | | | | | |
| EU27 | 1.08 | 1.86 | 1.07 | 0.78 | −0.02 |
| Old15 | 1.00 | 1.77 | 1.00 | 0.77 | 0.00 |
| New12 | 1.55 | 2.39 | 1.42 | 0.84 | −0.13 |
| Latin Arc countries | 1.24 | 2.02 | 1.28 | 0.78 | 0.03 |
| Spain | 1.71 | 2.58 | 1.83 | 0.87 | 0.12 |
| France | 0.83 | 1.56 | 0.80 | 0.73 | −0.03 |
| Italy | 1.32 | 2.07 | 1.35 | 0.75 | 0.03 |

shows a much lower per capita GDP trend than in the baseline scenario (Figure 4.4c). Interestingly, the expected aggregate macroeconomic trends presented in Chapter 3 (Section 3.5) receive empirical validation.

Table 4.7 presents the aggregate results for the main European aggregates as well as for three countries, belonging to the so-called 'Latin Arc', which will be the area of empirical simulation analysis in Part III. In the reference scenario, the MASST2 model projects a national GDP growth rate for the EU's 15 old member countries (around 2 per cent yearly) which is slightly lower than the one observed in the past 10 to 20 years, since, as expected, it absorbs the structural changes brought about by the crisis.

For the New 12, the reference scenario is more expansive than for the Old 15; but probably not as much as in the past, since its hypotheses are not specifically in favour of the new member states, whose convergence continues without being too strong. The performance of the Latin Arc countries is around the average of the EU15 countries. Yet some national differences emerge among the three countries, with the performance of Spain being slightly higher than that of France and significantly higher than that of Italy. Despite the homogeneous assumptions, the three countries behave differently because of their structural features.

The proactive scenario (A) is more expansionary for Europe as a whole, as well as for its countries individually. Eastern countries appear to benefit from this scenario slightly more than Western countries, because of higher FDI and stronger demand. Latin Arc countries still perform around the average of the EU15, with an average annual GDP growth rate which is 1 per cent above that of the reference scenario. The rankings among the three countries are unaffected by a courageous and anticipatory strategy scenario; Italy remains the worst-performing country, however, it gains an imperceptibly higher advantage from the assumptions of this expansionary scenario.

The results of the defensive scenario (B) are, as expected, significantly less expansionary with respect to both the proactive and the reference scenarios. The new member states continue to outperform the Old 15 countries, but convergence is much slower; a defensive attitude towards structural changes hits these countries particularly with respect to the rest of the EU. Latin Arc countries are as negatively affected as the rest of the EU in this scenario, and their performance is almost in line with that of the Old 15 member countries. It is interesting to observe that, although the relative rankings of the three countries in terms of average annual GDP growth rates remain the same as in the reference scenario, the country most negatively affected is Spain, although it is still the best performing of the three. Defensive strategies therefore appear particularly hard to sustain for countries which have developed a model of high growth through employment creation in the past.

In our scenarios, Spain turns out to be the country which changes its development trends most markedly with respect to the past: all three Latin Arc countries have always been rather closely synchronized in their cycles, so that recessions tend to hit them similarly. However, in periods of growth, Spain has normally outperformed both France and, especially, Italy in the 1990s and 2000s. But in recent times, Spain appears to have been hit by the economic crisis more strongly than France and is generally projected by EUROSTAT to exit from the crisis more slowly than the other two countries. As will be evidenced in Chapter 7, the baseline MASST result is likely and quite in line with other projections, as well as being plausible due to the different economic structures of the three countries.

Table 4.7 also presents the results for total employment growth rates (with the exception of agricultural employment), also divided between service and manufacturing employment growth rates. It is immediately evident that the reference scenario registers an increase in total employment; however, the increase is due to an increase in the service sector, while the expected re-launch of manufacturing activities in Europe through the development of the green economy is mainly driven by productivity increases. The increase in total manufacturing activities, in fact, is smaller than that in GDP. Among the three Latin Arc countries, Italy is the one that registers the lowest productivity increase, having in fact a higher increase in employment growth than France, but a lower increase in GDP.

Employment growth is evident in the service sector. It is larger in New 12 member countries with respect to Old 15; and this applies to service employment, which grows more, and for manufacturing employment, which decreases less.

The proactive scenario registers an increase of employment, with respect to the reference scenario, in services and in manufacturing. Because this growth rate is lower than the increase in GDP, it is evident that the proactive scenario also registers an increase in productivity with respect to the reference. The relative rankings of Old 15 and New 12 countries are respected, because the differences are almost the same. However, the additional employment created in the proactive scenario is more in services than in manufacturing, especially for New 12 countries.

The defensive scenario is very interesting. In fact, at European level, employment growth is almost the same as in the reference scenario; given the lower GDP growth rates, this scenario clearly evidences a loss in productivity, as expected. The defensive strategy, therefore, appears to be able to maintain employment levels at the same level of the baseline scenario, but this happens to the detriment of productivity.

Also very specific to this scenario is the fact that its employment growth is closely similar to the baseline at an aggregate level, but very different at regional level, as will be evident in Section 4.6, where it will be shown that the difference from the baseline is positive for some regions and negative for others.

## 4.5 REGIONAL GDP GROWTH RATES

The advantage of the MASST2 model is its ability to produce foresights for each NUTS-2 region of the EU. NUTS-2 quantitative foresights for the whole of Europe allow the prediction of economic growth rates under different scenarios for the various regions, at the same time taking account of:

- the macroeconomic conditions, which affect all Europe and the various countries, so that the growth rate of any region is not independent from that of its respective country and that of Europe; and
- the effects of regional interactions, since no region is a world apart but its growth rate also depends on its interactions with neighbouring regions (see Section 4.2.3).

The main output of the MASST2 model is the GDP growth rate for each NUTS-2 region of the EU27; and other regional outputs are the population growth rates and the employment growth rates. In this section, the results on the GDP growth rate are presented at the regional level, while the results for employment growth rates are shown in the next section.

In the reference scenario (Map 4.1), the GDP growth rates of European regions are highly differentiated, and the national results of Section 4.4 hide different patterns concerning different groups of regions. The growth rate is positive for all regions; but while some considerably outperform the others, the growth in the others is sluggish.

Consistently with the expectations of the qualitative integrated scenarios developed in Chapter 3, one can observe that growth within countries will be a centripetal process, with the strongest areas as the leaders in all countries. In Eastern Europe, all capital regions, such as Budapest, Sofia and Warsaw, are among the best performers overall, sometimes (as in the case of Prague, Bratislava and Bucharest) also pulling the regions adjoining them. Rural areas in the East are on the contrary sluggish, as are all rural areas around Europe, being affected by the deregulation of the Common Agricultural Policy (CAP) and increased international competition.

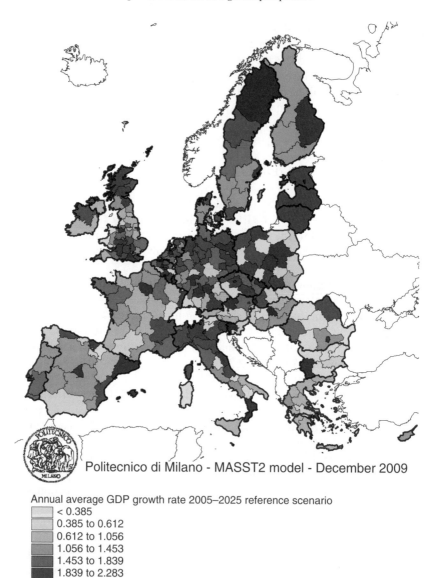

Politecnico di Milano - MASST2 model - December 2009

Annual average GDP growth rate 2005–2025 reference scenario
- < 0.385
- 0.385 to 0.612
- 0.612 to 1.056
- 1.056 to 1.453
- 1.453 to 1.839
- 1.839 to 2.283
- 2.283 to 2.793
- 2.793 to 3.576
- > 3.576

*Map 4.1    Annual average regional GDP growth rates in the reference
             scenario*

In the West, the first-ranked regions are those which generally outperform the others, as shown by the performances of areas such as Stockholm, Copenhagen, Munich, Frankfurt, Brussels, Lisbon and Athens. However, second-order areas are also thriving, as shown by the examples of Malmö, Hertfordshire (UK), Edinburgh and Ghent.

This pattern is confirmed within the Latin Arc countries. The highest growth rates within their respective countries are experienced by Île de France, Lombardy, Madrid and Catalonia, but very high growth rates can also be found in second-order economies, in regions such as Valencia, Rhône-Alpes, Piedmont and Emilia-Romagna. The performance of Languedoc-Roussillon is intermediate, being the outcome of differentiated areas within it.

The proactive scenario (Map 4.2) is more expansionary for all regions of Europe, both in the West and in the East. However, some regions benefit more than others. In the new member countries, the areas which perform better are the core and capital ones, the only areas endowed with the human capital and technological ability necessary to exploit the green economy paradigm (for example, Budapest, Prague and Warsaw).

Interestingly, especially in the West, it is not necessarily the first-level core regions that benefit more, but rather a number of second-level areas. For example, Poznan in Poland, a large number of intermediate regions in Germany, Bruges and Ghent in Belgium, and Porto in Portugal, all register a difference of annual GDP growth rate with respect to the reference scenario which is higher than their respective capitals. This result is in line with the qualitative speculations made in Chapter 3, in which conjectures were made on the development of production activities related to the green economy towards second- and third-level cities. Despite these spatial trends, this scenario is still one in which the absolute numbers show a centripetal pattern, a result confirmed by the analysis of regional disparities presented in Section 4.7.

With regard to the Latin Arc, in the proactive scenario the core regions also perform well, but the development spreads to second-order poles. In France, the good performance of Paris notwithstanding, Rhône-Alpes, Provence-Côte d'Azur, Haute Normandie, Bretagne and Pays de la Loire are the regions that take most advantage of the scenario. In Spain, Madrid and Barcelona show very good growth rates, but the greatest difference is reported in Valencia and Oviedo. In Italy, the spread of development to secondary growth poles is even more marked, with very high differences reported in Veneto and Campania (the region of Naples). Despite the good performance of second-order regions, however, rural areas do badly in this scenario, since they achieve a positive but consistently lower performance both in relative and in absolute terms.

*Spatial scenarios in a global perspective*

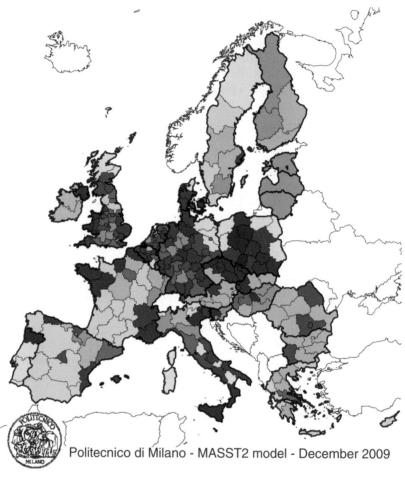

Politecnico di Milano - MASST2 model - December 2009

Annual average GDP growth rate 2005–2025 difference between scenario A and reference
☐ < 0.525
☐ 0.525 to 0.731
☐ 0.731 to 0.857
☐ 0.857 to 0.955
☐ 0.955 to 1.031
☐ 1.031 to 1.12
☐ 1.12 to 1.196
☐ 1.196 to 1.312
■ > 1.312

*Map 4.2    Annual average regional GDP growth rates: difference between
the proactive and the reference scenario*

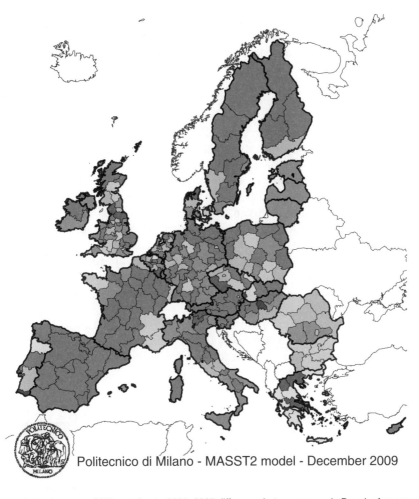

Politecnico di Milano - MASST2 model - December 2009

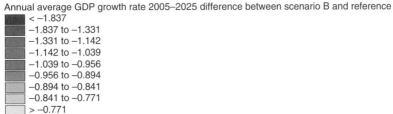

Annual average GDP growth rate 2005–2025 difference between scenario B and reference

- < −1.837
- −1.837 to −1.331
- −1.331 to −1.142
- −1.142 to −1.039
- −1.039 to −0.956
- −0.956 to −0.894
- −0.894 to −0.841
- −0.841 to −0.771
- > −0.771

*Map 4.3   Annual average regional GDP growth rates: difference between the defensive and the reference scenario*

The differences between the defensive and reference scenarios are reported in Map 4.3. This scenario is characterized by low growth rates, with development concentrated in the few highest-level metropolitan areas. The MASST2 model obtains the same results as theoretically induced in Chapter 3. As expected, this scenario is less expansionary with respect to the reference one for all regions of Europe. In particular, in the East, the regions more able to survive the recessions include some capitals, such as Bucharest and Sofia: especially in absolute terms, the growth rates in this scenario are significantly higher for Eastern metropolitan regions.

This is also the case of the Latin Arc countries. In Italy the best relative performance is that of Latium, whereas in France it is achieved by Provence-Côte d'Azur and Rhône-Alpes, but Paris is not the most negatively affected region. In Spain, the differences are less marked, but the regions better able to cope with the restrictive hypotheses are Madrid, Catalonia and Seville.

As a last consideration, this scenario does not favour rural areas. On the contrary, owing to lack of demand for their products, insufficient investment, and a decline in manufacturing, these regions lose more from this scenario.

The total level of European disparities increases in all three scenarios, but especially in the defensive scenario, in which only the most important metropolitan areas are able to react, and the weakest countries suffer most from the protectionist policy.

## 4.6  REGIONAL EMPLOYMENT GROWTH RATES

### 4.6.1  Regional Industrial Employment Growth Rates

The MASST2 model is also able to provide foresights for employment growth rates, separately for manufacturing and services. The annual average growth rates of manufacturing employment are represented in Maps 4.4 to 4.6.

The results of the reference scenario are not in line with the qualitative foresights. Contrary to what the latter envisage, negative manufacturing growth rates are registered in this scenario. The recovery of manufacturing activities expected to result from the launching of the green economy seems insufficient to counterbalance the negative manufacturing job effects of the recent crisis and the productivity increases put in place by the new technological paradigm of the green economy.

In Europe as a whole, the effects of a recovery of manufacturing activities are limited to some peripheral areas, while in general, negative growth

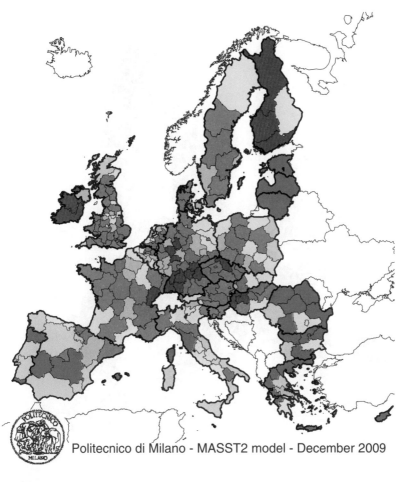

Politecnico di Milano - MASST2 model - December 2009

Annual average industrial employment growth rate 2005–2025 reference scenario

- −6.821 to −2.885
- −2.885 to −1.698
- −1.698 to −1.2
- −1.2 to −0.881
- −0.881 to −0.529
- −0.529 to 0
- 0 to 0.507
- 0.507 to 2.14

*Map 4.4    Annual average regional industrial employment growth rates in the reference scenario*

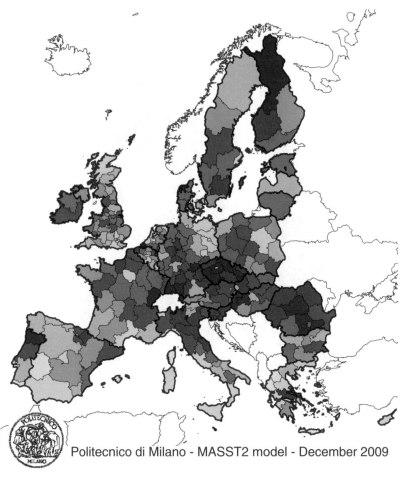

Politecnico di Milano - MASST2 model - December 2009

Annual average industrial employment growth rate 2005–2025 A - reference
- 0.007 to 0.079
- 0.079 to 0.135
- 0.135 to 0.177
- 0.177 to 0.209
- 0.209 to 0.248
- 0.248 to 0.288
- 0.288 to 0.345
- 0.345 to 0.439

*Map 4.5    Annual average regional industrial employment growth rates:
difference between the proactive and the reference scenario*

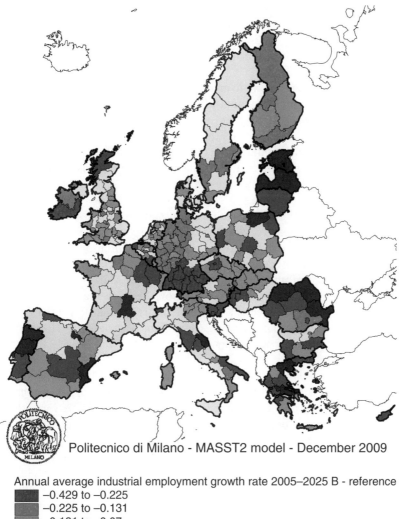

Politecnico di Milano - MASST2 model - December 2009

Annual average industrial employment growth rate 2005–2025 B - reference
- −0.429 to −0.225
- −0.225 to −0.131
- −0.131 to −0.07
- −0.07 to 0
- 0 to 0.006
- 0.006 to 0.047
- 0.047 to 0.099
- 0.099 to 0.224

*Map 4.6    Annual average regional industrial employment growth rates: difference between the defensive and the reference scenario*

rates of manufacturing employment are registered in most regions of Europe, especially in many traditional manufacturing regions of Central Europe, which shift towards the service sector. Moreover, in all countries the areas with large cities normally have negative values, often the lowest in their respective countries.

Manufacturing employment growth rates register a recovery in some regions of Bulgaria and Romania which, having joined the EU later than the other countries, still have an advantage in terms of manufacturing costs with respect to the rest of the Union. Moreover, slightly positive manufacturing employment growth rates are found in the Baltic countries, in the eastern Polish fringe, and in many western regions belonging to Objective 1, as well as in some areas characterized by the presence of small and medium-sized enterprises.

Map 4.5 depicts the difference in manufacturing employment growth rates between the proactive and the reference scenarios. For all regions of Europe, the proactive scenario is able to provide more manufacturing employment with respect to the reference scenario. In this scenario the re-launching of manufacturing activities in Europe through the development of the green economy is more decisive than in the reference scenario. This is especially so for many regions in Central Europe – German, Czech, northern Italian, Slovenian, Austrian and Hungarian – and no decisive differences appear between Old 15 and New 12 member countries.

Interestingly, the most important urban areas are not the main winners in this respect, probably because they tend to reinforce their advantage in the new economy and hence are likely to gain more in services than in manufacturing. Moreover, the Objective 1 areas in western countries, hosting manufacturing activities less advanced with respect to those in their respective countries, are less able to take advantage of this scenario and increase their manufacturing employment. Map 4.6 depicts the differences in manufacturing employment growth rates between the defensive and the reference scenarios. In this case, the situation is mixed, with many regions increasing and many regions decreasing manufacturing employment with respect to the reference scenario.

The most important observation is that, in the defensive scenario, defensive policies tend to benefit manufacturing activities that are not the most advanced ones, and consequently tend to be detrimental to those regions that are the richest ones. For this reason, negative values are registered in Germany, especially its southern part, as well as in most of Scandinavia, the United Kingdom and the richest regions of France, Italy and Spain.

Mediterranean regions often gain in manufacturing employment thanks to the defensive strategy, whereas the situation for New 12 member countries is mixed. Apart from Hungary and the Czech Republic, where all regions have negative values, all other countries seem to have a blend of positive and negative values, with some capital areas (such as Warsaw) with negative values and others (Bucharest–Iflov) with positive ones.

### 4.6.2 Regional Service Employment Growth Rates

The last important outcome of the MASST2 model to be presented is the service employment growth rate.

Map 4.7 depicts the case of the reference scenario, which has on average positive service employment growth; positive values are in fact more frequent and in absolute value significantly higher than negative ones. The results are especially positive for New 12 member countries, with the exception of Poland, and for Italy, Greece and Spain, which appear to continue their pre-crisis trend of service employment creation, not necessarily at a high level. In other countries, such as Portugal, the UK, France Sweden, Denmark, Belgium, Finland and Germany, service employment creation appears to be a characteristic of the most important urban areas, including Paris, London, Frankfurt, Brussels, Lisbon, Copenhagen, Stockholm and Helsinki, whereas other areas, mainly rural and/or peripheral, appear to slightly decrease their service employment. Also in those countries where service employment creation is higher, the most important urban areas appear generally to outperform the rest of the country, in cases such as Lombardy, Vienna, Madrid and Bucharest.

In the proactive scenario, whose difference from the reference one is depicted in Map 4.8, the service employment growth rate is larger for all regions of Europe. The assumptions on sectors make it especially positive for regions in New 12 countries, with the exception of Bulgaria and Romania, which, as we saw in Maps 4.4 and 4.5, are characterized by strong employment growth in manufacturing. Also in western countries, service employment growth appears to be positive for many peripheral areas, which have a more positive effect with respect to their countries.

The defensive scenario (Map 4.9) presents a situation of service employment growth which is very negative for many regions and slightly positive for other ones. In particular, negative values are registered by eastern regions, which, due to the defensive strategy, are unable to accomplish a transition towards the service economy and have to remain manufacturing economies. This is especially true for some eastern capitals (such as Budapest, Warsaw, Prague and Bucharest) which would miss the opportunities to transform themselves into real service cities. In western countries,

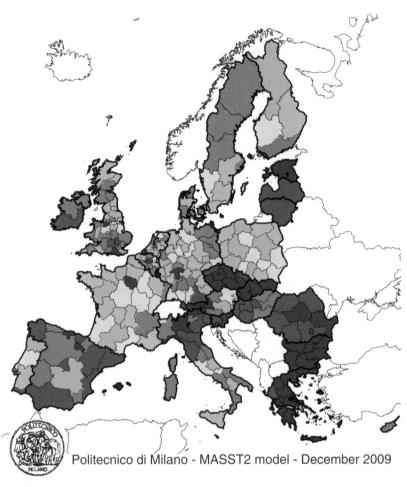

Politecnico di Milano - MASST2 model - December 2009

Annual average service employment growth rate 2005–2025 reference scenario
- −1.535 to −0.627
- −0.627 to 0
- 0 to 0.332
- 0.332 to 0.82
- 0.82 to 1.35
- 1.35 to 2.01
- 2.01 to 3.43
- 3.43 to 5.976

*Map 4.7    Annual average regional service employment growth rates in the
          reference scenario*

Politecnico di Milano - MASST2 model - December 2009

Annual average service employment growth rate 2005–2025 A - reference
- 0.564 to 0.641
- 0.641 to 0.692
- 0.692 to 0.739
- 0.739 to 0.795
- 0.795 to 0.859
- 0.859 to 0.935
- 0.935 to 1.06
- 1.06 to 1.317

*Map 4.8    Annual average regional service employment growth rates:*
*difference between the proactive and the reference scenario*

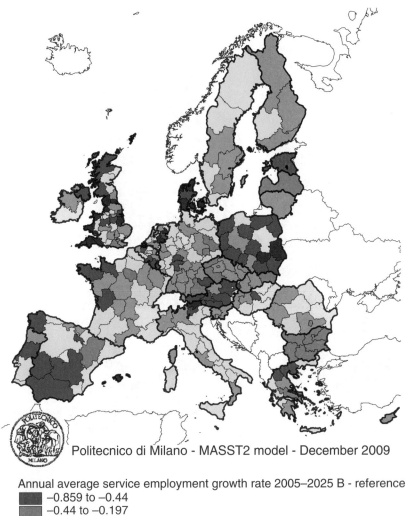

Annual average service employment growth rate 2005–2025 B - reference

| | |
|---|---|
| ■ | −0.859 to −0.44 |
| ■ | −0.44 to −0.197 |
| ■ | −0.197 to −0.058 |
| □ | −0.058 to 0 |
| □ | 0 to 0.145 |
| ■ | 0.145 to 0.225 |
| ■ | 0.225 to 0.324 |
| ■ | 0.324 to 0.47 |

*Map 4.9    Annual average regional service employment growth rates:*
*difference between the defensive and the reference scenario*

the defensive strategy appears to protect weak service sectors to the detriment of more advanced ones. In so doing, this strategy is often positive for the service employment of weaker regions and significantly negative for service-advanced regions, whose economic potential is not fulfilled, including Paris, London, Rome, Munich, Frankfurt, Berlin, Amsterdam, Copenhagen and Madrid.

## 4.7 REGIONAL DISPARITIES

The results of the MASST2 model can be used to analyse the trends of regional disparities in the three scenarios. This is done by compounding the Theil index, which makes it possible to disentangle the level of total disparities due to within-country disparities (that is, intra-national disparities between regions of the same country) or due to between-country disparities (that is, the disparities between the various countries of the EU). Both are plotted in Figure 4.5. The total level of European disparities increases in all three scenarios, and especially in the defensive scenario, where only the most important metropolitan areas are able to react, and weaker countries are often more negatively affected. Interestingly, this result contains an important message: a proactive strategy does not necessarily bring with it more disparities than a defensive strategy.

The two components of disparities show that between-country disparities decrease in all three scenarios, whereas the disparities within countries

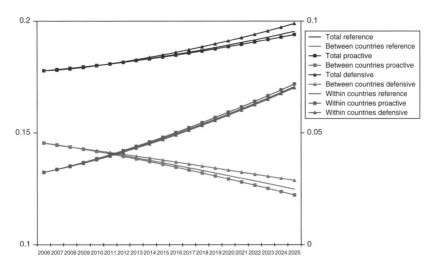

*Figure 4.5   Theil index of regional disparities in the three scenarios*

increase. In fact, we foresee in the three scenarios (see Table 4.7 presented before) higher growth rates for those countries (especially the new member states) which start with a lower GDP per capita. This is especially the case in the proactive scenario, where the growth rate is higher for all countries, but is especially higher for the eastern ones.

Within-country disparities (depicted on the right axis) are lower in size but, differently from between-countries disparities, they are expected to increase in all three scenarios, and slightly more so in the proactive one, where first- and second-level regions perform better than rural and peripheral ones.

The sum of the decrease of between-country disparities and the increase of within-country disparities determines the slight increase in total disparities.

## 4.8   CONCLUSIONS

This chapter has presented the new version of the MASST model, the so-called MASST2, which can produce quantitative foresights for all regions of Europe at NUTS-2 level over a time span of 10–20 years. The predictions of MASST2 are not predictions in the common meaning of the word, rather they are more the outcome of logical exercises and especially worthwhile for scenario exercises where the accent is put on the effects of the main bifurcations which could affect the world economy (and the European one in particular) in the future.

The results obtained by the MASST2 forecasts are in line with the speculations of the integrated scenarios in Chapter 3. The proactive scenario is the most expansionary of the three, and the defensive scenario is the least expansionary. However, not all countries benefit in the same way from a proactive scenario. In particular, it appears that the New 12 countries are those whose growth rate depends more on scenario assumptions, since their smaller economies are more affected by global trends.

Also, at regional level the differentiations are important. Even if all regions benefit in terms of GDP from a proactive scenario and all regions lose under a defensive scenario, the patterns of different types of regions are very different. Most agglomerated areas benefit from the proactive scenario more than do rural and peripheral areas; interestingly, the same agglomerated areas are not normally those that lose most from a defensive scenario, since they are better able to defend themselves under these tightened conditions. With regard to regional disparities, therefore, they increase in all three scenarios but especially in the defensive one, which suffers from the fact that New 12 countries lose more from it.

The results of the MASST2 model are of great interest for interpretation of the scenarios at spatial level; they are, however, still too broad to be used for policy measures at territorial level. It is therefore important to territorialize the results by scaling down to NUTS-3 level, and by explicitly adopting a territorial capital perspective. This will be done in the next chapters, which develop a sub-model, SPAN3, able to distribute the NUTS-2 regional growth rate of MASST2 among the NUTS-3 provinces belonging to a region.

## APPENDIX 4A1   THE EFFECTS OF ASSUMPTIONS ON VARIABLES IN MASST: SOME CAVEATS

In order to interpret the results of the scenarios correctly, three important caveats should be borne in mind. First, the absolute numbers have no real meaning but are only helpful in analysing qualitatively the trends induced by the assumptions. In fact, the qualitative assumptions are translated into quantitative values, that is precise numbers, so that they can be used in the model. The transforming of qualitative assumptions into numbers is done on the basis of learned judgement, and of comparison with past means and variances of the variables. Nevertheless, the actual numbers chosen maintain a degree of subjectivity, so that, for example, a diminishing growth rate of the BRICs' GDP is, in our assumptions, 2 percentage points less than the reference; but the scenario results would be almost the same if the decrease was instead 2.5 or 3 percentage points, only with slightly different numerical results.

Second, the model is not additive, and recursive effects occur. For this reason, the effects induced by a modification in two targets is never the sum of the effects of the modifications induced by each target separately; nor is the joint effect necessarily lower or higher than the two when separate. Moreover, the model is generative and distributive at the same time (see Section 4.2). Therefore, any modification in a regional target has two simultaneous effects: the first is on the country's growth rate, generating more or less growth depending on whether the new target is more or less expansionary; the second effect is a different distribution of the national growth rate to regions, depending on how they perform in the new target. For this reason, the regional effect of a modification in a target variable is not straightforward: if one target is reduced, its aggregate (national) effect is negative. However, when the reduction does not take place in the same proportion in all regions, the regions with lower reductions may even benefit, since they will be able to outperform the other regions of the country and, hence, gain a larger proportion of total national growth. This process is the model's counterpart to a real-world game taking place between regions which, voluntarily or otherwise, compete to attract national production factors and firms.

Third, spillovers are at play, so that the effects induced by a target modification on the growth of one region are due not only to the target of that particular region, but also to the targets of the neighbouring regions. Since spillovers affect regions differently with different spatial settings, the regional effects of target modifications are difficult to predict *ex ante*.

## APPENDIX 4A2 QUANTITATIVE LEVERS

*(a) Public expenditure, unit labour growth rate, real interest rates*

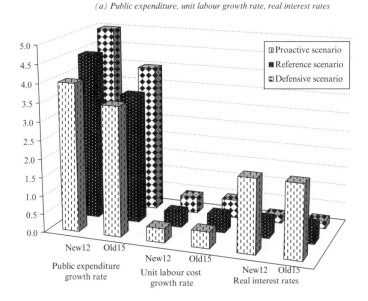

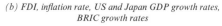

(b) *FDI, inflation rate, US and Japan GDP growth rates, BRIC growth rates*

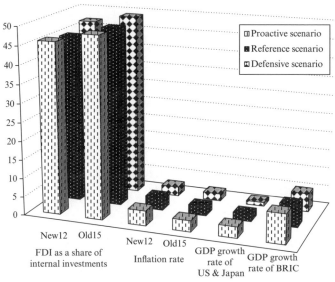

(c) *Exchange rates*

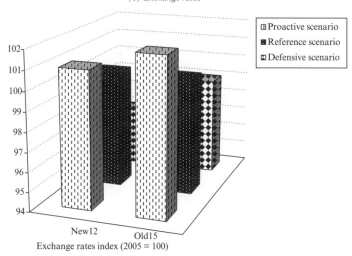

*Figure 4A2.1  National target values in the three scenarios (absolute values)*

*(a) Agglomerated and MEGA regions in Old 15 countries*

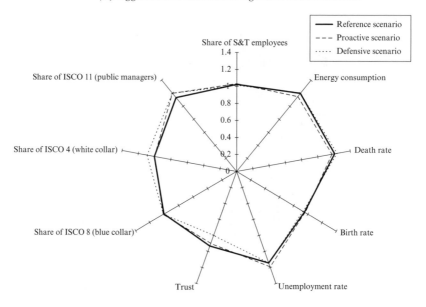

*(b) Urban and rural regions in Old 15 countries*

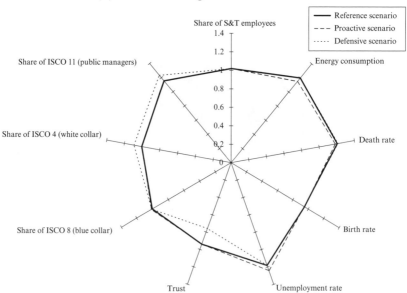

*(c) Agglomerated and MEGA regions in New 12 countries*

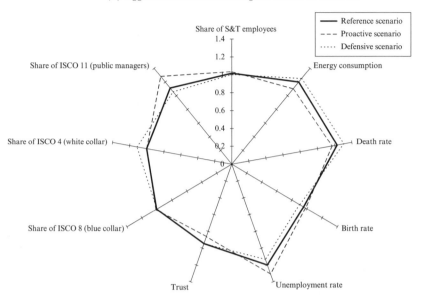

*(d) Urban and rural regions in New 12 countries*

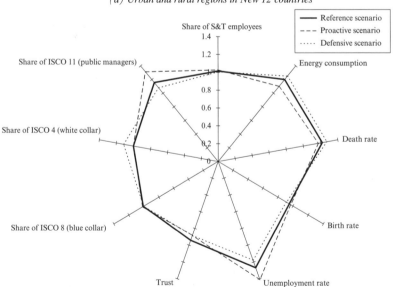

*Figure 4A2.2    Regional target values in the three scenarios (average group value in 2005=1)*

PART II

Scenarios at sub-regional level:
the Latin Arc countries

# 5. Quantitative foresights at sub-regional level: the model and estimation results

## Antonio Affuso, Roberto Camagni and Roberta Capello

### 5.1 MOVING FROM THE NUTS-2 TO THE NUTS-3 SCENARIO

The methodology presented in the previous chapter enables identification of scenarios at regional level. An additional step is required in order to build scenarios at a more disaggregated territorial level of analysis such as that of NUTS-3.

To this end, a simplified, extrapolative/comparative sub-model, the MAN-3 (MASST at NUTS-3) model has been implemented. The sub-model is conceived so that that the main trends and driving forces present in each scenario are considered and included in the forecasting process, as well as the importance of the territorial specificities of the individual regions of the countries considered. The way in which the MAN-3 sub-model is conceptualized makes it possible to replicate one of the most important characteristics of MASST; in fact, as in the case of the MASST model, the MAN-3 model aims at explaining the differential growth rates of each province with respect to its region on the basis of the structural characteristics and internal economic specificities of each area. The MAN-3 model is simpler than the MASST, in that the comprehensive interregional interaction logic of the latter (with the international inter-regional spillover effects) and its internal consistency among macroeconomic forecasts are not replicated in the MAN-3 sub-model.

The MAN-3 sub-model makes it possible to obtain the GDP growth rates at NUTS-3. Differently from MASST, the sub-model at NUTS-3 is able to produce only GDP growth, leaving aside employment and demographic forecasts. In this book, the model is estimated and applied to the provinces of the three countries of the Latin Arc: Italy, France and Spain.

The scenario methodology of combining the two models yields:

- a general and consistent scenario framework at NUTS-2, with a strong interlinkage among all regions of Europe made possible by the MASST model; and
- a 'fine-tuning' of the conditional foresights to the structural characteristics of each area made possible by the MAN-3 model.

As explained before, the most innovative aspect of MASST is that, by virtue of its simulation algorithm, it can be considered a 'generative' model of regional growth in the sense defined by Richardson (1969), even if it also encompasses macroeconomic and institutional aspects, which are typically national and top down. In MASST, regional growth has a role in determining national performance. The model thus supersedes the limiting and erroneous role given in general to the regional side of growth models: that of simply distributing national growth among regions by means of a typical top-down approach.

Differently from MASST, the MAN-3 model is a pure distributive model, in that it simply distributes regional growth among provinces of the same region using a typical top-down approach. The distributive nature of our model has a conceptual explanation. The endogenous capacity of local areas depends on the achievement of a critical mass of markets for final or intermediate goods, for input factors, and for service activities. When provinces are not strategic with respect to their region, their relatively small physical size prevents local economic activities from achieving a sufficient critical mass. When, on the contrary, NUTS-3 areas are strategic core areas for the region, able to explain through their dynamics most of the NUTS-2 growth patterns, the endogenous capacity for growth is already captured at NUTS-2 through the MASST model. In general, the achievement of a critical mass at local level is the result of close complementarity among economic activities in the different NUTS-3.

This conceptual approach is reflected in our models: the MAN-3 sub-model distributes regional growth among the provinces of each NUTS-2, while the MASST model captures complementarity effects among NUTS-3, thus modelling endogenous growth. Moreover, the MASST model takes account of synergy effects among NUTS-2 thanks to the presence of spatial spillovers (that is, the influence of each region on the growth trajectories of neighbouring regions). These factors determine the cumulative nature of regional growth patterns, as widely emphasized by the new endogenous growth theories and the 'new economic geography' rooted in Myrdal's and Kaldor's cumulative causation theory (Myrdal, 1957; Kaldor, 1970).

The forecasting exercise conducted with the MAN-3 sub-model comprised two distinct stages:

1. an *estimation stage* of the territorial factors that explain the relative growth of each NUTS-3 with respect to its NUTS-2; and
2. a *simulation stage* in which independent target variables are formulated and the NUTS-3 growth differential is simulated for the different scenarios.

In the estimation stage, the model explains the province's growth relative to the region through different components of territorial capital, such as infrastructure capital, sectoral specialities, natural resources, cognitive resources (human capital), and social capital. As in the case of MASST, this model interprets local growth with the help of the most advanced theories on local growth, without denying the importance of the achievements accomplished by the traditional theories, adding intangible elements such as cognitive and social factors *à la* Putnam to traditional material assets. The choice of the variables is also instrumental to the scenario assumptions and therefore to the levers necessary to run the simulation.

The simulation stage is based on the adjustment of the qualitative assumptions of the scenarios to the changes in the levels of the model. The differential growth rate at provincial level ($\Delta diff\, y_p^{MAN-3}$) obtained by the model is added to the regional growth model obtained from MASST ($\Delta y_r^{MASST}$), thus simulating the provincial growth rate ($\Delta y_p$):

$$\Delta y_p = \Delta y_r^{MASST} + \Delta diff\, y_p^{MAN-3} \,; p \in r. \qquad (5.1)$$

The next section presents the estimation model, together with the empirical results. The simulation assumptions and results are dealt with in the next chapter.

## 5.2 THE MAN-3 SUB-MODEL: TERRITORIAL ASSETS AND SPATIAL HETEROGENEITY

The factors explaining the relative performance of a sub-regional area reside in its *territorial capital*, a general concept that, as mentioned, covers all the genetic aspects of local growth.

In particular, the territorial capital assets included in the model should comprise traditional assets such as transport infrastructure, and intangible assets, in line with the new local growth theory, while not denying the role of sectoral specificities of individual provinces. The local characteristics to be covered reflect the need to take different types of territorial assets into account, namely:

- *infrastructure capital*, which includes physical accessibility;
- *productive capital* in the form of specialization in different economic activities, such as the presence of service or manufacturing activities, and tourism activities;
- *cognitive capital* in the form of knowledge, competences, skills, educational and research structures embedded in both productive and human capital;
- *social and relational capital* in the form of both civicness and associative capabilities; and
- *cultural and identitarian capital* encompassing cultural heritage, landscape and natural capital.

In principle, there is likely to be a positive correlation between positive economic growth and the territorial capital endowment. However, the relationship between the different assets of territorial capital and local performance is strongly mediated by territorial specificities. The presence of large cities, rural areas, or even natural resources provided by the geographical position, such as the presence of the sea, represents *per se* a richness for a local area, and a potential for its growth. At the same time, these territorial specificities require and strengthen particular aspects of the territorial capital in a cumulative and self-reinforcing process; agglomeration economies may influence the role of human capital on local performance through knowledge spillover effects, while the specialization in service activities may have a greater effect on local performance in agglomerated areas, where a larger service market is guaranteed, or in tourist areas characterized by a high demand for services.

These territorial specificities assume greater importance at a more disaggregated territorial level of analysis, and they call for an empirical analysis that takes account of the fact that the components of territorial capital may play a different role in areas characterized by specific natural resources and settlement structures. In other words, account must be taken of spatial heterogeneity, and this, regardless of the form that it takes, is a conceptual rather than a technical problem. In an empirical exercise, spatial heterogeneity can be easily resolved by using a regression model to test the restriction of uniform coefficients across NUTS-3 belonging to the same or to different NUTS-2.

However, this optimal strategy is rather costly in terms of degrees of freedom.[1] Given the lack of the latter, a second-best solution was chosen

---

[1]   From a technical point of view, this requires the inclusion in the regression equations of two sets of dummy variables: the first set consists of one dummy variable for each NUTS-3, while the second is made up of NUTS-2 dummy variables, as well as possible interacted effects.

and applied in the analysis reported here. In order to test the role played by spatial heterogeneity in the economic performance of provincial areas, two sets of dummies were used, one measuring the territorial specificities related to the urban settlement structure of the NUTS-3 areas (agglomerated, urban, rural, depending on the presence of cities with a certain density and size of population; and MEGA areas, depending on the presence of cities where high-value functions are located),[2] and the other capturing the geographical position and the presence of natural resources such as coastal or mountain areas.

These dummies were added in our econometric model first on their own. In a second stage they interacted with the other explanatory variables in order to test whether the estimated coefficients varied across types of provinces. This strategy makes it possible to assess, on the one hand, whether provinces with a particular territorial specificity are, *ceteris paribus*, more dynamic than other kinds of provinces, and, on the other hand, whether territorial assets explaining local performance have different impacts on growth according to the degree of territorial specificity of local economies.

For this reason, the MAN-3 sub-model aims at identifying the reasons why a sub-regional area is able to grow more or less than its region through the analysis of the role played by different types of the territorial assets and by territorial specificities.

The base model estimated was therefore the following:

$$\Delta y_p - \Delta y_r = \alpha_0 + \beta_1 \, infcap_p + \beta_2 cogcap_p + \beta_3 soccap_p + \beta_4 prodcap_p$$

$$+ \, \beta_5 cultcap_p + \alpha_1 D_{setstr_p} + \alpha_2 D_{geopos_p} + \varepsilon_p \qquad (5.2)$$

where *infcap* is the infrastructure capital, *cogcap* is the cognitive capital, *soccap* represents the social capital, *prodcap* is the productive capital and *cultcap* measures the cultural capital. *Dsetstr* and *Dgeopos* are categorical variables, the former equal to 1 if province $p$ is an agglomerated, an urban, a rural or a mega area, and zero otherwise; the latter equal to 1 if province $p$ is either a coastal or a mountain province, and zero otherwise.

The two kinds of dummies were then interacted with the other explanatory

---

[2]   The settlement structure variables are defined as those in the MASST model. Agglomerated provinces are defined as those provinces with a city of > 300,000 inhabitants and a population density > 300 inh./km sq. or a population density 150–300 inh./km sq.; urban provinces are defined as those provinces with a city of between 150,000 and 300,000 inhabitants and a population density 150–300 inh./km sq. (or a smaller population density–100–150 inh./km sq. with a bigger centre (>300,000) or a population density between 100 and 150 inh./km sq.; rural provinces as provinces with a population density < 100/km sq. and a centre > 125,000 inh. or a population density < 100/km sq. with a centre < 125,000.

variables. This strategy made it possible to assess, on the one hand, whether agglomerated areas, for example, are, *ceteris paribus*, more dynamic than other kinds of regions, and, on the other, whether territorial assets have different impacts on growth according to the type of provinces we encounter.

The model estimated therefore becomes:

$$\Delta y_p - \Delta y_r = \alpha_0 + \beta_1 \, infcap_p + \beta_2 cogcap_p + \beta_3 soccap_p + \beta_4 prodcap_p$$

$$+ \beta_5 cultcap_p + \alpha_1 D_{setstr_p} + \alpha_2 D_{geopos_p} + \alpha_3 D_{setstr_p}$$

$$* \sum_{i=1}^{5} X_{ip} + \alpha_4 D_{geopos_p} * \sum_{i=1}^{5} X_{ip} + \varepsilon_p, \tag{5.3}$$

where $D_{setstr}$ and $D_{geopos}$ are categorical variables, and $X_{ip}$ is the vector of the five types of explanatory variables which can affect relative provincial growth, as discussed when describing equation (5.2).

A last conceptual question was whether the territorial capital assets explaining the performance of a local area are similar in the three countries analysed, or whether there exist 'national models of local development' based on some specific structural assets for each country. For this reason, the differential provincial growth rates were analysed country by country, so that similarities and differences among territorial assets explaining local performance among countries emerged. An integrated interpretative model of local performance for all three countries was estimated in a subsequent phase, where the main explanatory territorial assets of each country were used. A single estimation model allowed the same parameters to be used in the simulation exercise for the Latin Arc countries. In the integrated model, national specificities in local development models were taken into consideration through dummy variables.

## 5.3 THE DATABASE: TERRITORIAL ASSETS AND SPECIFICITIES INDICATORS

The MAN-3 sub-model is dependent on the existence of a consistent and large database, which comprises two types of data measuring the different territorial capital assets on the one hand, and the territorial specificities on the other.

A first degree of complexity in building such a database derives from the fact that good proxies must be chosen as indicators in order to grasp the different elements of territorial capital assets, the infrastructural, productive, cognitive, social and cultural capital. Another cause of complexity, and of limitation in the possible choice of proxies for the territorial capital assets, is the fact that the data must be available for all NUTS-3 of the three countries from the same source, so that they can be used in the same econometric model. For this reason, the data sources selected were European sources. The data collected came from EUROSTAT, ESPON[3], and the NSD (Norwegian Social Science Data Survey) European Election Database, and they covered the total NUTS-3 of Spain, Italy, and France excluding its overseas departments.

EUROSTAT was the source for economic performance data. The dependent variable was the relative provincial GDP growth rate with respect to the region, and it was measured by the difference between NUTS-3 and the NUTS-2 GDP growth rates in real terms in the 2001–05 period, computed from the nominal rate using national GDP deflators. The ESPON and NSD databases were the sources of the proxies for the territorial capital assets.

According to the elements of territorial capital, the explanatory variables were grouped into the above-mentioned five sets of factors: infrastructure capital, productive capital, cognitive capital, social and relational capital and cultural and identitarian capital (Table 5.1).

*Infrastructure capital* was proxied by:

● the share of road infrastructure, calculated as the difference between the average share of km of road at NUTS-3 level and the average share of km of road at NUTS-2 level, in the 1986–96 period.

The second set of factors was related to *productive capital* and contained:

● the share of service employment, a variable useful to capture the role of services in explaining economic performance. We expect to find that this variable positively affects the provincial performance because the service sector is on average more value-added than manufacturing, in the year 2001;
● the share of industrial employment, in the year 2001; and
● the share of tourism facilities: given the geographic position and vocation of the Latin Arc countries it is not possible to leave tourism and its impact aside. We measured the impact of tourism through

---

[3] The ESPON 2013 Programme, the European Observation Network for Territorial Development and Cohesion, supports policy development related to EU Cohesion Policy by developing territorial analyses and collecting territorial data. Data from ESPON were downloaded from the 2006 database version, and data from the EUROSTAT database during the autumn of 2009.

*Table 5.1    The dependent variable and territorial capital assets indicators*

| Indicators | Variable | Source of raw data |
|---|---|---|
| *Dependent variable* | | |
| GDP growth rate of province with respect to its region | GDP growth rate at NUTS-3 in real terms in the period 2001–05, computed from the nominal one, using national GDP deflators | EUROSTAT |
| *Infrastructure capital* | | |
| The share of road infrastructures | Km of road infrastructure/surface, 1986–96 | ESPON DATABASE |
| *Productive capital* | | |
| The share of services employees | Employment in services/total employment in 2001 | EUROSTAT |
| The share of manufacturing employees | Employment in manufacturing/total employment in 2001 | EUROSTAT |
| The share of tourism facilities | Total tourism facilities/surface in 2001 | EUROSTAT |
| *Cognitive capital* | | |
| The share of people aged under 20 | People aged under 20/population in 2001 | EUROSTAT |
| The share of migratory balance | Migratory balance/population, 1996–99 | ESPON DATABASE |
| The share of high value-added functions | High value-added functions (calculated as the sum of ISCO 1, ISCO 2, and ISCO 3)*/total employment in 2001 | EUROSTAT |
| *Social and relational capital* | | |
| The growth of the electoral turnout rate in European elections | The growth rate of electoral turnout in European elections in the 1994–99 period | NSD EUROPEAN ELECTION DATABASE |
| *Territorial settlement structure and geographical position dummy variables* | | |
| Agglomerated areas | With a city of >300,000 inhabitants and a population density of >300 inhabitants/sq. km or a population density of 150–300 inh./sq. km | ESPON DATABASE |
| Urban areas | With a city of between 150,000 and 300,000 inhabitants and a population density of 150–300 inh./sq. km or a smaller population density of 100-150 inh./km with a bigger centre (>300,000) or a population density between 100 and 150 inh./sq. km | ESPON DATABASE |

*Table 5.1*   (continued)

| Indicators | Variable | Source of raw data |
| --- | --- | --- |
| Rural areas | With a population density <100/sq. km and a centre >125,000 inh. or a population density <100/sq. km with a centre <125,000 | ESPON DATABASE |
| MEGA areas | Regions in which is located at least one of the 76 'MEGAs' – functional urban areas with the highest scores on a combined indicator of transport, population, manufacturing, knowledge, decision-making in the private sector | ESPON DATABASE |
| Coastal areas | Areas located on the coast | ESPON DATABASE |

*Note:*   * ISCO 1 = legislators, senior officials and managers; ISCO 2 = professionals; ISCO 3 = technicians and associate professionals.

the share of tourism facilities per $km^2$ at NUTS-3 level, in the year 2001. Our expectation was that it positively affects province differential growth.

The third set of factors, namely *cognitive capital*, consisted of:

- the proportion of people aged under 20, a proxy for potential future human capital which should positively affect economic performance. In fact, young people are the most dynamic part of the population and ensure the bases for economic growth. This variable measured the share of people aged under 20 at NUTS-3 level in 2001;
- the migratory balance, which shows the attractiveness capacity of the territory: a positive migratory balance provides an adequate labour force to successful provinces with low fertility rates. It is measured by the share of migratory balance on population at NUTS-3 level, 1996–99. This variable, too, was expected to show a positive impact on economic growth; and
- the high-level value-added functions, proxied by the share of managers and professionals at NUTS-3 level, in the year 2001.

A proxy for *social capital* elements was used, namely:

- the growth of the participation rate in European elections. Although it is not easy to find good variables for social capital, some indirect measures have been proposed in the literature (Putnam, 1993). In our case, this variable was used as an indicator of civic duty and active engagement with public issues. It was calculated as the growth rate of electoral turnout in European elections at NUTS-3 level, in the 1994–99 period. The expectation was that the civic duty would prove to be positively correlated with economic growth.

The settlement structure and the geographical position of NUTS-3 were captured by the following dummies for:

- coastal provinces;
- rural provinces;
- urban provinces;
- agglomerated provinces; and
- 'MEGA' (MEtropolitan Growth Areas) provinces.

The ways in which these dummies were calculated are reported in Table 5.1. The dummies were inserted in equation (5.1) to determine whether they followed particular development trajectories, and in equation (5.2) to capture spatial heterogeneity.

Finally, a system of cultural elements and values which attribute sense and meaning to local practices and structures and define local identities should be considered because they can boost the internal capacity to exploit local potentials. Unfortunately, to our knowledge, homogeneous variables for the three countries able to describe the system of cultural elements and values which attribute sense and meaning to local practices and structures and define local identities are not available. For these reasons, in our econometric exercise we were not able to include the cultural and identitarian capital elements.

All variables, both dependent and independent, were inserted in the model in differences with respect to their average regional values.

## 5.4 TERRITORIAL CAPITAL ASSETS FOR THE THREE COUNTRIES: ESTIMATION RESULTS

In the econometric exercise, the model was estimated first country by country, and then for the three countries of the Latin Arc as a whole. This section presents the results for the three countries of the Latin Arc (Table 5.2). For each country, variables explaining the differential growth rates of provinces with respect to their region were selected. The results show that the factors explaining the differential growth rates differ among countries.

Table 5.2   Estimations of the MAN-3 model, country by country[+]

| | France | | | Italy | | | Spain | | |
|---|---|---|---|---|---|---|---|---|---|
| | Mod. 1 | Mod. 2 | Mod. 3 | Mod. 1 | Mod. 2 | Mod. 3 | Mod. 1 | Mod. 2 | Mod. 3 |
| *Infrastructure capital* | | | | | | | | | |
| The share of road infrastructure | | | | | | | 4.092** | | 2.988* |
| *Productive capital* | | | | | | | | | |
| The share of services employees | | | 1.222 | | | | 6.801** | | 5.923** |
| The share of tourism structures | −0.083*** | −0.091*** | −0.097*** | −0.424*** | −0.415*** | −3.489** | | | −0.573 |
| *Cognitive capital* | | | | | | | | | |
| The share of people aged under 20 | | | | 26.473*** | 25.246*** | 16.985 | 11.333*** | | 8.774** |
| The share of migratory balance | 1.411*** | 1.664*** | 1.576*** | | | | 0.652** | | 0.863*** |
| The share of high value-added functions | | | | 4.387* | 8.050** | 9.544** | | | |
| *Social and relational capital* | | | | | | | | | |
| The growth of the electoral turnout rate in the European elections | | | | | | | 3.439** | | 3.571** |

Table 5.2 (continued)

| | France | | | Italy | | | Spain | | |
|---|---|---|---|---|---|---|---|---|---|
| | Mod. 1 | Mod. 2 | Mod. 3 | Mod. 1 | Mod. 2 | Mod. 3 | Mod. 1 | Mod. 2 | Mod. 3 |
| *Territorial settlement structure and geographical position dummy variables* | | | | | | | | | |
| Rural areas | | −0.294* | −0.279 | | | | | | |
| MEGA areas | | | | | −0.759* | −0.816* | | | |
| *Spatial heterogeneity* | | | | | | | | | |
| Tourism structures endowment in Spanish rural provinces | | | | | | | | 16.439* | |
| People aged under 20 in Spanish 'agglomerated' provinces | | | | | | | | 33.415*** | |
| Service employment in French coastal provinces | | | −5.110* | | | | | | |
| Tourism structures endowment in Italian 'agglomerated' provinces | | | | | | 3.058** | | | |
| People aged under 20 in Italian 'agglomerated' provinces | | | | | | 36.017** | | | |

| | | | | | | | | |
|---|---|---|---|---|---|---|---|---|
| Constant | -0.047 | 0.052 | 0.053 | 0.018 | 0.080 | 0.065 | -0.133 | -0.113 |
| Number of obs | 96 | 96 | 96 | 95 | 95 | 95 | 41 | 41 |
| $F_{(2, 93)}$ | 47.21 | 38.31 | 28.09 | 15.23 | 12.06 | 12.07 | 12.53 | 12.42 |
| Prob > F | 0.00 | 0.00 | 0.00 | 0.00 | 0.00 | 0.00 | 0.00 | 0.00 |
| R-squared | 0.124 | 0.157 | 0.1744 | 0.123 | 0.1389 | 0.202 | 0.5607 | 0.6417 |
| Root MSE | 0.71034 | 0.70063 | 0.70102 | 1.0009 | 0.99727 | 0.97088 | 0.66803 | 0.63095 |
| Spatial error: | | | | | | | | |
| Moran's I | | | 0.486 | | | 0.500 | | -0.371 |
| Lagrange multiplier | | | 1.342 | | | 0.724 | | 0.410 |
| Robust Lagrange multiplier | | | 0.183 | | | 0.227 | | 0.196 |
| Spatial lag: | | | | | | | | |
| Lagrange multiplier | | | 2.316 | | | 0.553 | | 0.997 |
| Robust Lagrange multiplier | | | 1.157 | | | 0.056 | | 0.783 |

*Notes*

\* Significant at the 10% level; \*\* significant at the 5% level; and \*\*\* significant at the 1% level.

+ Spatial autocorrelation in our OLS results is tested for using Moran's I and Lagrange multiplier tests and the hypothesis that spatial autocorrelation exists can be rejected.

*Table 5.3    Estimations of the MAN-3 model for the Latin Arc countries*

|  | Latin Arc |
|---|---|
| *Productive capital* | |
| The share of services employees | 0.441 |
| The share of industries employees | −4.197** |
| The share of tourism structures | −0.111*** |
| *Cognitive capital* | |
| The share of people aged under 20 | 0.01 |
| The share of migratory balance | 1.496*** |
| The share of high value-added functions | 6.522*** |
| *Social and relational capital* | |
| The growth of the electoral turnout rate in the European elections | 0.014 |
| *Territorial settlement structure and geographical position dummy variables* | |
| MEGA areas | −0.361** |
| *Spatial heterogeneity* | |
| Touristic structures endowment in Spanish rural provinces | 27.878*** |
| People aged under 20 in Spanish 'agglomerated' provinces | 47.820*** |
| Service employment in French coastal provinces | −4.452* |
| The growth of the electoral turnout rate in the European elections in Spanish provinces | 3.573*** |
| People aged under 20 in Italian 'agglomerated' provinces | 71.836*** |
| Constant | −0.043 |
| Number of obs | 223 |
| F( 2, 93) | 25.34 |
| Prob > F | 0 |
| R-squared | 0.2471 |
| Root MSE | 0.8123 |
| Spatial error: | |
| Moran's I | 0.297 |
| Lagrange multiplier | 1.117 |
| Robust Lagrange multiplier | 0.034 |
| Spatial lag: | |
| Lagrange multiplier | 1.273 |
| Robust Lagrange multiplier | 0.191 |

Once identified, these elements were used to explain the Latin Arc as a whole. Indeed, the goal was to develop scenarios for the entire area and not for each country. The results obtained were generally in line with our expectations.

Our methodology to estimate the effects of territorial capital on each country was divided into three steps (Table 5.3). In the first one, we used the components of the four sets of factors: infrastructure capital, productive capital, cognitive capital, and social and relational capital. We did not use elements of cultural and identitarian capital for the reasons given above. In this way, we identified the main factors explaining the differential growth rates. In the second step, we added the territorial settlement structure and geographical position dummy variables to control for the influence of these variables on territorial performances. In doing so, we started from the well-known idea that the territorial and geographical structure should be taken into account when seeking to explain the economic performance of a territory. Finally, we controlled for spatial heterogeneity by means of the interactions between the elements of territorial capital and the territorial settlement structure and geographical position dummy variables. This control is important because *spatial heterogeneity* represents the effects of geographic patterns on regional economies and generates economic behaviours unstable over space. This three-step procedure also enabled us to check for the robustness of the model. Indeed, inspection of the significance of the coefficient shows that it changes only in two cases. In particular, with regard to the French models the coefficient of the dummy 'rural' is no longer significant in model 3; and with regard to the Italian models, the share of young people is significant in models 1 and 2, but not in model 3.

Finally, we tested the spatial autocorrelation for each country using Moran's I and Lagrange multiplier tests, and the hypothesis that spatial autocorrelation existed could be rejected. More specifically, the tests for spatial autocorrelations were run on model 3 of each country, which represented the final model of the entire Latin Arc.

The spatial autocorrelation test was made for scientific rigour, but it was expected to be absent. The model, in fact, was measured with variables calculated as differences with respect to the regional average; similarities among provinces within the same regions were drastically reduced. Spatial autocorrelation could have been possible between provinces belonging to different regions, but the spatial autocorrelation tests proved that this was not the case.

### 5.4.1 France

On analysing the elements of territorial capital in French provinces, the importance of cognitive capital in explaining the differential growth rates emerges. In fact, migratory balance is the only element with a positive and significant impact. The importance of this factor is confirmed by the stability of its coefficient, which is positive and significant in all models. This result reinforces the idea that immigrant labour generates income for the host areas. Particularly in a context of rapid population ageing, where demographic factors may act as a constraint on labour markets, in-migration plays an important role in driving economic growth.

Of some interest is also the negative and significant sign of service employment in French coastal provinces, which is probably correlated with the negative impact of the endowment of tourism facilities. This latter presents a negative and significant coefficient in all models, even though it is small.

The impact of the dummy 'rural' is not stable. Indeed, as we said before, it changes its significance in model 3.

### 5.4.2  Italy

Also in Italy, cognitive capital is the main factor explanatory of province differential growth rates through the share of young people and the share of high-level functions. Moreover, the spatial heterogeneity elements also play a role.

The territorial structure is fundamental in explaining differential growth rates and also in diversifying the impact of several elements. Indeed, the dummy 'MEGA' is negative and significant, showing that agglomeration economies and network effects do not emerge, although possible problems of excessive crowding and congestion arise.

Variables interacted with the dummy 'agglomerated' show strongly significant and positive effects. In Italy, too, the endowment of tourism facilities is negative and significant. In spite of the positive effect of the variable multiplied by the dummy 'agglomerated', indicating a positive effect of urban tourism, the overall effect remains negative.

On analysing cognitive capital, it was found that the share of people aged under 20 has a positive effect on province differential growth rates. This is due to the stagnation of demography and the intensification of the ageing process, which also affect the role of young people in economic growth. In fact, young people constitute a competitive advantage, because they are the most productive part of the population. As model 3 shows, this is particularly true in agglomerated provinces.

With respect to high-level functions, our results show that these positively influence the differential growth rate of a province compared to its region, supporting the hypothesis that high-level functions play a major role in economic growth.

### 5.4.3 Spain

Differently from the other two countries, the territorial elements explaining differential growth rates in Spain belong to all four sets of factors.

Transport infrastructure also plays an important role in the case of Spain. Our results show that road infrastructures positively affect the differential growth rates of Spanish provinces. This result is in line with, for example, the findings of Holl (2004), who finds that in a country such as Spain, where the motorway network has only recently been developed, and where considerable inter- and intraregional differences exist, access to road transport infrastructure plays an important role in manufacturing plant location, and that motorways affect the spatial distribution of new manufacturing establishments by increasing the attractiveness of areas close to the new infrastructure.

In contrast to the other countries of the Latin Arc, in Spain, and in the Catalonia region in particular, the young age of the population (sustained natural growth and positive migration balance) favours further population increase and limits the decrease of the ageing process. Indeed, between 2000 and 2008, average population growth was above 1.5 per cent per year only in Spain and two other EU member states. In this regard, we found that, also in the case of Spain, young population age has a positive and significant effect on the differential growth rate, as well as on the migratory balance.

The result for service employment shows a significant and positive influence on GDP. The positive sign is indubitably linked to the present economic shift to the service sector.

The growth rate of participation in European elections is not significant in Italy and France, but it is strongly significant and positive in Spain. This factor is probably linked with the positive economic growth of Spain.

The effect of the share of tourism facilities is interesting because it is unexpectedly strongly positive in rural Spanish provinces, probably showing the existence of a new type of tourism far from cities and close to the natural environment.

It is remarkable that the territorial structure does not play any role.

### 5.4.4 Comments

One important message arises from the results. Latin Arc countries exhibit marked 'national models of development' characterized by different elements of territorial capital and by different territorial specificities that in some cases reinforce the effects of specific territorial capital elements in their effects on local dynamics.

This first step consisting in the country-by-country analysis allowed us to highlight the most important variables to be considered for a model of all three countries together. The existence of 'national models of development' suggested that dummies for countries should be inserted in the general estimated model. The move towards the general model enabled us to obtain higher degrees of freedom and to achieve greater explanatory capacity of the model. The next section presents the results for the general model estimated on the Latin Arc as a whole.

## 5.5   TERRITORIAL CAPITAL ASSETS FOR THE LATIN ARC: ESTIMATION RESULTS

The final model for the Latin Arc was built starting from the 'country' models in order to consider the significant territorial capital elements of each country. The idea was to generate a model that took account of the diversities among France, Italy and Spain but treated the Latin Arc as an independent entity, also with specific territorial features. The general fit of the model was acceptable, having a 0.25 per cent of the variance explained. This result is satisfactory given that a differential shift in growth rates is explained.

Usually, the spread of globalization generates a twofold effect on the productive capital of a local area. On the one hand, if manufacturing activities are coupled with an urban or metropolitan environment (second-rank cities and metropolitan areas), there appears to be a strong positive effect on total growth rates. Evidently, these territories are the best suited and equipped to manage globalization processes with success. On the other hand, the effect is weaker in manufacturing areas with low or intermediate technologies and a relatively high labour intensity. This twofold effect seems to be partially captured by our results, showing that the share of industrial employment has a negative effect overall.

The result on service employment is quite surprising because it has a non-significant influence on GDP growth in the Latin Arc. This variable multiplied by the dummy 'coastal' in French provinces remains negative and significant in the French model as well.

In recent years, tourism has become an important engine of growth owing to enhanced international openness, booming geographical mobility, cheap air fares and rising income levels in many countries. Unexpectedly, the endowment of tourism facilities is negative and significant. The variable multiplied by the dummy 'rural' in Spanish provinces assumes important explanatory power, indicating a new appeal of rural areas. In Italy, too, the endowment of tourism facilities is negative and significant. In spite of the positive effect of the variable multiplied by the dummy 'agglomerated', indicating a positive effect of urban tourism, the overall effect remains negative.

With regard to cognitive capital, as expected, we found that the migratory balance has a positive and significant effect, while the share of people aged under 20 does not matter in the Latin Arc as a whole. Nevertheless, the latter is particularly important in explaining the differential growth rates in 'agglomerated' provinces, both in Italy and in Spain. This result shows the power of second-rank cities in attracting the most dynamic and productive people.

An interesting result is linked to the share of high value-added functions. In fact, it is strongly positive and significant in the Latin Arc, confirming that the most dynamic areas are those with a strong presence of high value-added functions (Affuso et al., 2011).

The results on the social and relational capital are not satisfying. The reason is linked to the shortage of variables at the NUTS-3 level, but also to the economic stagnation and the political framework, especially in Italy. With regard to Spain, the result of the 'country' model is confirmed by multiplying the participation growth rate with the dummy country.

Finally, as in Italy the dummy 'MEGA' is negative and significant, showing diseconomies of agglomeration.

## 5.6   CONCLUSIONS

In this chapter we have described a new econometric model at the provincial level that explains differential growth rates of provinces with respect to their regions according to territorial specificities (that is, territorial capital) by transferring the logic and operation of the MASST model (Capello, 2007; Capello et al., 2008; Capello and Fratesi, 2009) from the regional to the province level.

The factors that explain the relative performance of a sub-regional territory consist in its territorial capital, which covers all genetic aspects of local growth. Territorial capital may be seen as the set of localized assets – natural, human, artificial, organizational, relational and cognitive – that constitute the competitive potential of a given territory (Camagni, 2009; Camagni and Capello, 2009 and 2010).

Accordingly, the explanatory variables were grouped into five sets of factors: infrastructure capital, productive capital, cognitive capital, social and relational capital and cultural and identitarian capital.

The analysis was run on the provinces of the Latin Arc countries, France, Italy and Spain. In particular, the model was estimated first country by country separately, and then for the three countries of the Latin Arc as a whole. Our findings have shown that the Latin Arc is not a homogeneous space, and that the elements of territorial capital explaining the differential growth rates among the three countries are different. Indeed, although these three countries are considered to be similar in their characteristics, they are deeply different in the territorial elements explaining differential growth rates. Treatment of the Latin Arc as a homogeneous space should take this issue into account.

# 6. Quantitative foresights at sub-regional level: assumptions and simulation results

**Antonio Affuso and Ugo Fratesi**

## 6.1 INTRODUCTION

The previous chapter estimated an econometric model for the GDP growth rate of all provinces (NUTS-3) of three countries of the European Union: France, Italy and Spain. This model, MAN-3, is especially helpful in the development of scenarios at provincial level, as will be shown in this chapter.

In particular, the MAN-3 model can be used to obtain much finer scenarios at a territorial level than that of Chapter 4. In fact, while MASST has 265 European NUTS-2 regions, MAN-3 has only 232 NUTS-3 provinces belonging to the three countries, which have in total just 60 NUTS-2 regions. The level of spatial disaggregation is hence about four times finer and allows the production of results that are better able to take account of territorial specificities.

As mentioned in Chapter 5, however, the MAN-3 model is purely distributive, while the MASST2 is distributive and generative at the same time. This is due to the fact that provinces are too small to contain internally all of the assets needed to enable endogenous growth, and for this reason they rely much more closely on interaction with each other. Hence, growth must be determined at a higher, regional, level, rather than at provincial level. Provinces, however, also compete with each other to appropriate parts of growth that are generated by all of them together.

This requires the close integration of the MASST and MAN-3 models in the development of scenarios, since the former is able to produce regional growth rates and the latter is able to distribute this growth among the provinces of which a region is composed in order to produce scenarios at a finer territorial level.

The starting point of any scenario exercise at provincial level, therefore, must be a scenario already developed at regional level. In our case, the starting point for developing scenarios at provincial level with MAN-3 are the three scenarios theoretically developed in Chapter 3 and then empirically developed with MASST2 in Chapter 4. Methodologically speaking, therefore, the scenarios at provincial level need to start from the scenario values devised for scenarios at regional level and, if GDP growth is the target variable, from the MASST2 scenario GDP growth rates.

Because the provincial growth model is distributive, identification of scenario assumptions at provincial level must follow a procedure different from that at regional level, which, as was shown in Chapter 4, involved the use of regional target values. The procedure for targets at provincial levels, on the contrary, involves the variance of the variables, as will be illustrated in Section 6.2.1.

The logic of the scenario assumptions, however, will be the same as that of the scenarios of Chapter 3, and it will plot them on a different set of variables, those of MAN-3, in a way that will be presented in Section 6.2.2.

It will hence be possible to produce scenarios at NUTS-3 for France, Italy and Spain perfectly consistent with the European scenarios developed in Chapter 4. The results of the scenarios at provincial level will be presented in Section 6.3.

## 6.2 CONVERTING QUALITATIVE SCENARIOS INTO QUANTITATIVE ASSUMPTIONS AT PROVINCIAL LEVEL

### 6.2.1 The Differential Logic in the Implementation of Scenarios at Sub-regional Level

As explained in Chapter 5, provinces are not endogenously able to determine their growth rates, although their interaction is capable of determining the endogenous push of growth at regional level. This is why the MAN-3 model estimated a provincial growth differential without any recursive aspect or any effect from national components.

It is hence clear that, unlike in the case of MASST, it is not possible to use MAN-3 to produce autonomous scenarios; rather, another model must be used at a higher geographical level. As expressed in equation (5.1) of Chapter 5, the actual growth rate of provinces, in fact, must be expressed by the equation:

$$\Delta y_p = \Delta y_r^{MASST} + \Delta diff\, y_p^{MAN-3}; \; p \in r, \tag{6.1}$$

where $\Delta Y_p$ is the provincial growth rate, which is equal to the regional growth rate obtained by MASST ($\Delta y_r^{MASST}$), plus the provincial shift ($\Delta diff y_p^{MAN-3}$).

Estimations are obtained with all provinces at the same time; in estimations the weight of each province is the same, despite their size being different. Moreover, in the scenarios it is possible to change exogenous variables. For both reasons, the values in equation 6.1 may not be consistent with the ones at regional level: for example, the weighted sum of the growth rates of provinces in a region ($\Delta Y_p; p \in r$) may not add up to the regional growth rate ($\Delta Y_r$).

To resolve this inconsistency, a rescaling of the provincial growth rates is necessary so that their relative rankings are unaffected and consistent values are obtained. The easiest way to do this is to work through the levels and determine the final provincial growth rate of the scenarios as follows:

$$\Delta Y_{p2005-2025} = (Y_{p2025}/Y_{p2005})^{\frac{1}{20}}, \tag{6.2}$$

where:

$$Y_{p2025} = Y_{p2005} * (1 + \Delta Y_{r2005-2025}^{MASST} + shift_{p2005-2025}^{MAN-3})^{20}$$

$$* \frac{Y_{r2025}^{MASST}}{\sum_{p \in r} Y_p^{2005} * (1 + \Delta Y_{r2005-2025}^{MASST} + shift_{p2005-2025}^{MAN-3})^{20}}.$$

Equation (6.2) hence provides the variable at the basis of the provincial scenario results which will be presented in Section 6.3.

The fact that the MAN-3 model is distributive also has implications for the procedure used to identify target values for the different scenarios. It is in fact impossible to reason in terms of changes in the absolute values of exogenous variables through targets in 2025, as was done for the MASST model. This procedure would, in fact, risk generating no effect on the scenarios, since all provinces of the same region would often change in the same direction.

Moreover, the MAN-3 model involves variables that are related to structural elements of the local economies, which are supposed to change very slowly; thus it is very unlikely that the rankings in these variables of provinces of the same region could change. The solution chosen is to adopt a procedure based on the differences among provincial endowments rather than on their absolute values. This is consistent with an estimation which is based on differential growth, and it works as follows.

Each exogenous variable of the MAN model, multiplied by its coefficient, produces an effect on the provincial shift. If some provinces are more endowed with a certain variable than are other provinces of the regions, and if this variable has a positive coefficient in the estimations, then it will have a positive effect on the provincial shift. If some provinces are more endowed with a certain variable but this variable has negative coefficients in the estimations, then it will have a negative effect on the provincial shift.

Assuming that provinces do not change their ranking in terms of structural variables, which is plausible given the structural nature of these variables, what will change in the scenarios is the importance of a certain variable for the provincial growth.

The provincial specification of scenarios will hence be characterized by the differing importance assumed by the endowment of territorial capital variables in different scenarios, which can be achieved in two alternative ways:

- by enlarging/reducing the variance of a certain variable, which requires assumptions on whether provinces will become more or less similar in this scenario on that territorial variable; and
- by increasing/decreasing the values of the coefficient of a certain variable, which requires assumptions on whether the endowment of that variable will be more or less important for growth in the scenario.

Technically, however, the two ways are equivalent, which makes it possible to place more emphasis on the first interpretation in those cases where endowments are considered to be changing, or more emphasis on the second interpretation in those cases in which a variable is believed to play a key role in provincial competitiveness in a certain scenario.

### 6.2.2   From Qualitative Assumptions to Quantitative Levers

The variables that were included in the estimations of Chapter 5 can be used in order to simulate scenarios in the model. For logical consistency, each variable is affected by only one trend, in a way described in the first two columns of Table 6.1, which present the quantitative levers of the MAN-3 sub-model for each qualitative assumption.

First, the share of service employment, which has a positive sign, is a good proxy for simulating the qualitative assumption of the increase in service activities in the global economy and the increase in the advanced economic functions, which are concentrating more and more in metropolitan regions.

*Table 6.1    Qualitative assumptions and levers of the MAN-3 model*

| Qualitative assumptions | Quantitative levers of the model | Effects of the scenarios | | |
|---|---|---|---|---|
| | | Reference | Proactive | Defensive |
| Increased service activities in the global economy and in the advanced economic functions concentrating | Share of service employment | Positive impact | Highly positive impact (especially provinces with MEGAs) | Neutral impact |
| more and more in metropolitan regions | Share of manufacturing employment (negative coefficient) | Negative impact | Highly negative impact | Neutral impact |
| The green economy and the recovery of manufacturing activities in Europe | High-level functions | Positive impact | Positive impact | Negative impact |
| Effects of the crisis on tourist regions | Endowment with tourism structures (negative coefficient) | Negative impact | Negative impact (but less than in the reference) | Neutral impact |
| Deregulation of the CAP and trade liberalization in the context of the WTO | Rural regions | Negative impact | Negative impact | Neutral impact |
| Difficulties for regions affected by the housing crisis | Regions specialized in construction | Negative impact | Negative impact | Negative impact |
| Stagnation of European demography and intensification of the ageing process | Share of people aged under 20 | Positive impact | Negative impact | Strong positive impact |
| Immigration flows from the Mediterranean Basin to Latin Arc countries | Migratory balance | Positive impact | Positive impact | Negative impact |
| Diffusion of economic development in urban areas | Urban provinces | Neutral impact | Positive impact | Neutral impact |
| | Agglomerated provinces | Neutral impact | Neutral impact | Positive impact |

The recovery of manufacturing activities in Europe, which is strictly dependent on the development of the green economy, is translated in the model scenarios through the share of high-level workers, given that these represent a good proxy for the provincial specialization in high-level functions fundamental for the competitiveness of the manufacturing sector.

The endowment with tourism structures is a very good proxy for simulating the effects which the economic crisis has induced on tourism regions.

Trade liberalization, due to possible agreements in the context of the World Trade Organization (WTO) and the possible deregulation of the Common Agricultural Policy (CAP), will affect rural provinces differently from the other ones. Since a 'rural' dummy variable is not present in the estimations, in this case we had to use a different procedure and work through the constant as if there were a dummy for provinces specialized in rural activities estimated with coefficient 0, which can, however, increase or decrease in the scenarios.

Like the above-mentioned one, the constant coefficient for regions specialized in the construction sector can represent the different difficulties experienced in the scenarios by the different provinces because of the housing crisis.

The internal demographic processes, especially the stagnation of European demography and the intensification of the ageing process, are represented in the scenarios through the variable of people aged under 20, which depends on the demographic processes and which has a very small and very insignificant, though positive, sign in the estimations, with the exception of Spanish agglomerated provinces, which register a large and positive sign.

On the other hand, the hypotheses on the immigration flows from the Mediterranean Basin to the Latin Arc countries, are translated through the migratory balance variable, which is positive and represents the attractiveness of regions.

Finally, the scenarios also involve assumptions on the spatial structure of the European territory: in particular, the diffusion of economic development, which may be concentrated in the most agglomerated areas or diffused to second-order cities (urban provinces) or also towards the more dispersedly settled rural provinces. This is captured by the respective dummies.

As is evident, not all aspects of territorial capital are included in the estimations, since some levers that would be desirable are not present at NUTS-3 level owing to data availability or for econometric reasons. A possible solution to this problem will be provided in Chapter 7 when the 'fine-tuning' procedure is presented.

A further step towards the construction of scenarios at NUTS-3 is the adaptation of the scenario assumptions defined at European level for the province level, using the levers which have been just described.

In the reference scenario, the spread of globalization into regions helps the recovery of manufacturing activities in Europe. The process has a twofold effect. On the one hand, there is an increase in manufacturing activities due to significant technological progress. This is to the advantage of developed regions, second-rank cities and metropolitan areas, although the effect is weaker in manufacturing areas with low or intermediate technologies and a relatively high intensity of manpower. On the other hand, given the recovery of manufacturing activities, the increase in the service activities of the economy slows down. However, services still have a positive effect on economic growth. These processes are translated by a larger importance of manufacturing specialization for growth. Since the share of manufacturing employment has a negative sign and the share of services employment has a positive one, this implies that the impact on the coefficient is positive for services and negative for manufacturing.

Although the competition for stronger increases in service activities is attenuated, the proactive scenario is characterized by a movement towards higher added-value segments and the resurgence of higher financial services, which are particularly concentrated in MEGA cities. Therefore, in this scenario, provinces with a higher share of service employment grow more than the region as a whole, and provinces containing MEGA cities even more so, which translates into a highly positive effect on those regions.

In the defensive scenario, these effects are weaker because new service activities are mainly concentrated in and around metropolitan areas, so that medium-sized and smaller cities where low-profile businesses, such as call centres, are largely represented, are particularly affected. The competitiveness of activities of this type declines because of insufficient adjustments and productivity-related investments.

For these reasons, in the simulation exercise the share of service employment positively influences the differential growth rate of a province compared to its region in a way similar to that found in the estimations, that is, less than in the reference scenario.

The effects of the green economy are captured by the share of high-level functions, which is a good proxy for the ability of regions to move towards new technologies. The development of the green economy is typical of the reference scenario, but it is even more rapid in the proactive one. The new 'paradigm' creates jobs in R&D and manufacturing activities, and it also generates new opportunities for entrepreneurship in non-agricultural rural regions. In the defensive scenario, having high value-added functions is less important, since the green economy does not achieve a breakthrough and hinders the development of alternative activities in the production of renewable energy. Investments in this field remain dispersed and insufficiently profitable. In this scenario, the non-emergence of the green economy depends on insufficient public support and modest mobilization by economic actors and civil society.

In the MAN model the share of craft and related trade workers has a positive role in distributing regional economic growth; a role which, in the light of the above-mentioned developments of the green economy, is increased in the reference scenario, is even greater in the proactive one, and is less important in the defensive scenario where having high value-added functions guarantees less growth. Moreover, these effects are amplified in non-agricultural rural regions in the proactive and the defensive scenarios.

In the reference scenario, the numerous tourism areas affected by the crisis show slow recovery, especially those based on mass tourism with low added value. Indeed, tourism is very volatile, and the recovery of these regions depends upon the general level of the European economy. Furthermore, the macroeconomic framework particularly affects the purchasing power of specific groups, such as low-income earners, because inflation and real interest rates increase and the growth of real income is modest. This implies that areas with more extensive tourism infrastructures are harder hit by the crisis. To reproduce this effect in the simulation, the impact of the endowment of tourism structures in each province is hit by a negative shock to change the distribution of regional economic growth among the provinces. This mechanism also works in the defensive scenario, where the stagnating European economy handicaps the development of tourism functions as well as the residential economy along the Latin Arc.

In the proactive scenario, the transition from carbon-related energy systems towards a new energy paradigm based more on renewable energy sources encourages a new tourism. Also the creation of the 'Union pour la Méditerranée' (UPM) may positively affect tourist flows. Overall, the positive economic climate favours provinces with tourism structures. This is beneficial to small and medium-sized cities, as well as to rural areas with an attractive natural and cultural heritage. In the proactive scenario, therefore, the endowment of tourism structures contributes positively to distributing regional economic growth across provinces.

Agriculture is undergoing a slow transition process towards more sustainable forms. Accordingly, the strengthening of policies supporting the further development of renewable energy sources is of great importance for the future of numerous rural areas. Furthermore, agricultural activities will be significantly influenced by the further liberalization of the CAP and the growing importance of extra-European competition.

In the reference scenario, evolution in rural areas is contrasting and heterogeneous. Some rural areas benefit from the production of renewable energy, but political support is insufficient to generate a radical change of the energy paradigm. Consequently, the progress of renewable energy sources remains dispersed and fragmented, with low synergy effects. Other factors influence the future of rural areas; particularly provinces specialized in agriculture are negatively affected by CAP reform and trade liberalization in the context of the WTO.

In the proactive scenario, a significant number of rural areas benefit from the diffusion of renewable energy sources, and the positive economic climate favours the development of rural areas with an attractive natural and cultural heritage. Nevertheless, all these elements do not offset the negative impact of the further liberalization of agriculture. In particular, rural agricultural regions are still negatively affected, because recovery from the crisis is rapid and favours manufacturing activities.

This is all the more true in the defensive scenario. Although the effects of CAP reform and trade liberalization are slower, and rural provinces maintain a protection, a significant number of rural regions are faced with serious problems of decline in agricultural yields which is not offset by the development of alternative activities such as the production of renewable energy. For these reasons, rural provinces specialized in agriculture are expected to be negatively affected by the general framework in the proactive scenario, highly negatively affected in the reference scenario, and neutrally affected in the defensive one.

Provinces which had booming activities in the building and construction sector, largely based on speculation in the real estate, have been particularly hard hit by the economic crisis and are also particularly penalized in the reference scenario. Even if there is favourable economic development, in the proactive scenario urban construction expansion remains contained. In the defensive scenario the stagnating economy handicaps the development of the residential economy. Moreover, second-level cities and medium-sized towns benefit much less from development because most of them are affected by the decline of manufacturing activities. For these reasons, the negative effect of construction specialization persists in the proactive as well as in the reference and the defensive scenarios.

The stagnation of European demography and the intensification of the ageing process also affect the role of young people in economic growth. An endowment of young people is a competitive advantage because they are the most productive part of the population and those most able to implement new technologies. This means that a province with a higher share of young people than other provinces has a greater share of regional growth, especially with the intensification of the ageing process.

In the reference scenario, the number of the 'oldest old' increases significantly. In the defensive scenario the European population even declines in the long run. In the proactive scenario, instead, fertility rates revive. In order to highlight these assumptions in the simulation model, the share of young people positively contributes to redistributing economic growth in the reference scenario, and even more so in the defensive one, while its impact is less important in the proactive scenario.

Immigration, in a context of rapid population ageing where demographic factors may act as a constraint on labour markets, plays an important role in driving economic growth. In the reference scenario, immigration is mainly concentrated in metropolitan areas, but also in areas attractive to tourists and retirees. In the proactive scenario, economic growth and the creation of significant numbers of new jobs foster the immigration of qualified manpower, particularly to large cities. In the defensive scenario, the slow recovery from the economic crisis negatively affects migration flows. Interregional migrations are more intense than in the reference scenario and benefit large cities, but they accelerate the urban sprawl and also exacerbate social tensions, in particular where unemployment is significant. Moreover, illegal immigration continues because of unfavourable economic conditions in North Africa and slow progress in the UPM.

Although the impact of migration is rather heterogeneous in the three countries, the migratory balance always has a positive weight in redistributing economic growth in the estimations. In the scenarios, the hypotheses are reflected by a larger importance of the provincial ability to attract foreign workers in the reference and proactive scenarios, especially with regard to agglomerated areas, whereas the exception is the defensive scenario, where immigration is less favourable to growth.

The last relevant aspect to be considered is the settlement structure of regions because the diffusion of the urban fabric and the use of land differ among the scenarios. In the reference scenario, the urban structure remains about the same as at present, with the same spatial division of economic activities between first- and lower-level cities. In the proactive scenario, growth is diffuse and spills over from the core areas to secondary poles, which are able to accommodate the activities which cannot be concentrated in the central areas, whereas provinces without poles are unable to attract them because of their weak structure. For this reason, in the proactive scenario growth is larger in the second-order cities (that is, urban provinces) and remains the same elsewhere.

On the other hand, in the defensive scenario, growth is centripetal and only the most agglomerated areas are competitive and attractive for economic activities. Hence, in this scenario, agglomerated areas are those that grow differentially more, because having a large agglomeration is the only way to have opportunities.

## 6.3 SIMULATION RESULTS AT NUTS-3 LEVEL

This section reports the growth rates of provinces in the three scenarios and compares rates between the proactive and reference scenarios and the defensive and reference scenarios. Because all results are calculated as in equation (6.1), they reflect the scenario assumptions of MASST, which were developed in Chapter 4, as well as the scenario assumptions of MAN-3, developed in Section 6.2.2 above.

Table 6.2 presents the average provincial growth rate in the three scenarios, reporting the results for the three countries of estimations (that is, France, Spain and Italy) since the growth rates of the rest of Europe are not available at provincial level. Consistently with the results of MASST (Table 4.7), the growth rate of Spanish and French provinces is higher than the average of the Latin Arc countries, whereas the growth rate of Italian provinces is the lowest in all scenarios. The differences among the impacts of the scenarios on the three countries are small. The proactive scenario is slightly more favourable to Italy, whereas the defensive scenario has a more negative impact on France.

The Latin Arc provinces are normally less dynamic than their countries, but they have a similar positive effect from the proactive scenario and a similar negative effect from the defensive one. Their settlement

*Table 6.2    Average provincial GDP growth rates 2005–2025*

|  | Reference | Proactive | Defensive | Difference between proactive and reference | Difference between defensive and reference |
|---|---|---|---|---|---|
| *All countries* | | | | | |
| All provinces | 1.96 | 2.94 | 0.98 | 0.98 | −0.98 |
| Spanish provinces | 2.06 | 3.02 | 1.02 | 0.96 | −1.04 |
| French provinces | 1.99 | 2.97 | 1.02 | 0.97 | −0.97 |
| Italian provinces | 1.83 | 2.83 | 0.89 | 1.00 | −0.95 |
| *Latin Arc Countries* | | | | | |
| All provinces | 1.73 | 2.69 | 0.77 | 0.96 | −0.96 |
| Urban provinces | 1.70 | 2.51 | 0.69 | 0.81 | −1.01 |
| Agglomerated provinces | 1.88 | 2.98 | 0.96 | 1.10 | −0.92 |
| MEGA provinces | 2.03 | 3.17 | 1.12 | 1.14 | −0.90 |
| Rural provinces | 1.11 | 1.88 | −0.01 | 0.77 | −1.13 |
| Coastal provinces | 1.84 | 2.89 | 0.90 | 1.05 | −0.94 |

structure appears to impact significantly on provincial performance, as evidenced by the fact that, in the reference scenario, urban provinces are slightly less dynamic than the average, and agglomerated regions, and especially those with MEGAs, are much more dynamic. Rural provinces appear to grow less than the average, whereas coastal provinces grow more.

Also the differential impacts of the scenarios are differentiated among provinces according to their settlement structures. In particular, agglomerated provinces, and especially those with MEGAs, appear to be at the same time those that gain more from a proactive scenario and those which lose less from a defensive one.

As can be observed from the maps, the general patterns hide provincial specificities. In the reference scenario (Map 6.1), the growth rates of European provinces are highly differentiated, and some provinces even register slightly negative growth. With regard to the typology of the provinces, agglomerated provinces benefit more than the others from this scenario, while rural provinces have the lowest growth rates.

By and large, peripheral rural and urban provinces, in particular those of the South and the North-West of Spain, the South-West of France, and the South of Italy are the worst performers. By contrast, provinces with MEGAs generally outperform the others. Overall, provinces specialized in building and constructions also have below-average growth rates. However, MEGAs benefit more than the others from this sector. The growth rate of tourism provinces is higher than average. In this respect, it is interesting to note that rural provinces specialized in tourism grow twice as fast as other rural provinces.

Although the agglomerated provinces show a positive trend, some interesting facts emerge from an in-depth analysis. Growth rates are lower than the average for all agglomerated provinces in the South of Italy, and for Seville, Zaragoza and Malaga. Moreover, growth rates are above 3 per cent only in Novara, Gorizia, Rimini, and in the French provinces of Yvelines, Essonne, Hauts-de-Seine, Seine-Saint-Denis and Val-de-Marne. Quite surprisingly, there are no Spanish agglomerated provinces above 3 per cent. With regard to other types of province, Spanish rural provinces have a higher growth rate than the other rural provinces, and the Italian provinces are the best performers among urban provinces.

It is also interesting to note that development spreads outwards from Barcelona, Paris and Milan to neighbouring provinces, which in many cases grow more rapidly. This is probably explained by congestion pushing activities towards second-rank cities with similar services and generating a low-cost housing market in the peripheries of large cities. This is

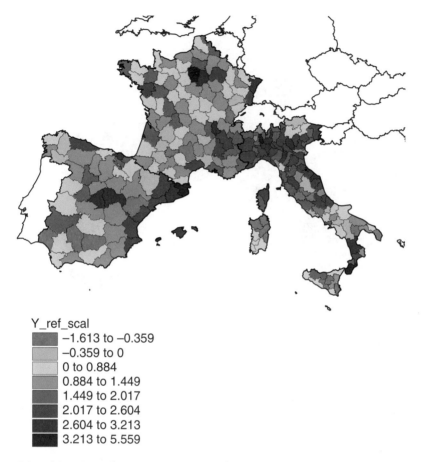

Y_ref_scal
- ■ −1.613 to −0.359
- □ −0.359 to 0
- □ 0 to 0.884
- ▨ 0.884 to 1.449
- ▨ 1.449 to 2.017
- ▨ 2.017 to 2.604
- ■ 2.604 to 3.213
- ■ 3.213 to 5.559

*Map 6.1    Annual average GDP growth rates, 2005–2025: reference scenario*

true only in part for Madrid and Rome, which grow more than their surrounding provinces.

The proactive scenario differs in many respects from the reference scenario and shows higher growth levels for almost all provinces. The differences between the proactive and the reference scenarios in terms of growth rates are shown in Map 6.2. Provinces exhibiting large differences between the proactive and reference scenarios include Rome, Madrid, and other MEGAs such as Barcelona, Valencia, Rhône Alpes, Milan and Bologna. Provinces with lower rates of growth normally occur around MEGAs. This is the case of the provinces surrounding Paris, Milan and Rome, and also Bologna, Naples and Vizcaya. This happens because during the first

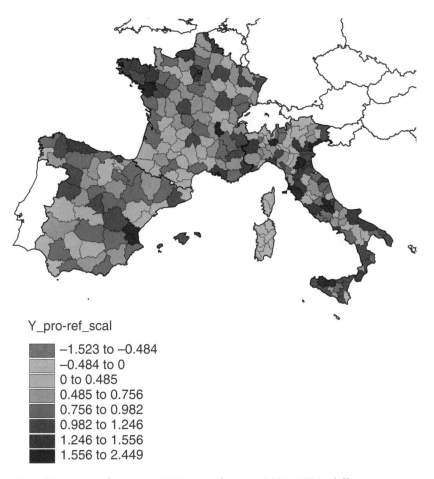

Y_pro-ref_scal

| | |
|---|---|
| ■ | −1.523 to −0.484 |
| □ | −0.484 to 0 |
| ▨ | 0 to 0.485 |
| ▨ | 0.485 to 0.756 |
| ■ | 0.756 to 0.982 |
| ■ | 0.982 to 1.246 |
| ■ | 1.246 to 1.556 |
| ■ | 1.556 to 2.449 |

*Map 6.2    Annual average GDP growth rates, 2005–2025: difference
between the proactive and the reference scenario*

phase (5 to 7 years) of the proactive scenario, growth is concentrated in metropolitan areas thanks to significant investments in advanced technologies. In a subsequent phase, green economy production activities spread towards second- and third-level cities and also towards the more peripheral provinces.

In general, Spanish provinces benefit more than the others from the proactive scenario. While in the reference scenario agglomerate provinces achieve the best performance, in the proactive these are the MEGAs. Moreover, differently from the reference scenario, the French urban provinces outperform the Italian ones.

Interestingly, some provinces with a low rate of growth in the reference scenario benefit more from the proactive scenario. This is the case, for example, of some Italian provinces in the Sicily region, the French provinces in the Franche-Comté region and Hautes-Pyrénées, Gers, Tarn-et-Garonne, Indre-et-Loire and the Spanish provinces of Lugo, Asturias, Teruel, Salamanca, Zamora, Cuenca, Eivissay Formentera, Mallorca, Menorca, Vizcaya, Madrid, Valencia and Barcelona. Many of these provinces are rural or urban. This shows that, as well as agglomerated provinces and capitals, the proactive scenario also favours those rural provinces hosting the development of the residential and tourism economy and the green economy, especially in the field of renewable energy sources (bio-mass, solar and geothermal energy and so on).

In the defensive scenario, the most heavily penalized provinces are the rural ones, which have an average rate of growth negative and close to 0. In fact, in the defensive scenario, a significant number of rural regions are faced with serious problems of declining yields in agriculture and job losses in small, no longer competitive, manufacturing industries. Moreover, the new paradigm of the green economy sustaining the growth of rural provinces which emerges in the proactive scenario does not emerge in the defensive one. Nevertheless, some rural provinces with a smaller difference in growth rates between the proactive and reference scenarios also show a smaller negative difference between the defensive and reference scenarios. This indicates that they are not particularly penalized by the defensive scenario.

Another interesting finding emerges on comparing the difference in growth in each scenario for each province with the average for all provinces (see Map 6.3). This reveals that some provinces exhibiting an above-average difference in growth in the proactive scenario compared to the reference one also have a below-average difference of growth rate in the defensive scenario. This indicates that these provinces both benefit more from the proactive scenario and are more badly affected by the defensive one. This is the case of several provinces close to agglomerated provinces. It is due to the fact that in the proactive scenario they benefit from the growth of big cities that spread outwards, but in the defensive scenario, where the growth of big cities is more self-contained, they grow to a lesser extent. More generally, provinces showing a positive trend in the proactive scenario tend not to lose out so heavily in the defensive one.

Among the provinces less affected by a defensive scenario are Paris and some provinces of Latium around Rome. The most affected are some provinces close to the largest cities, such as Guadalajara (close to Madrid), and many provinces of Île-de-France around Paris.

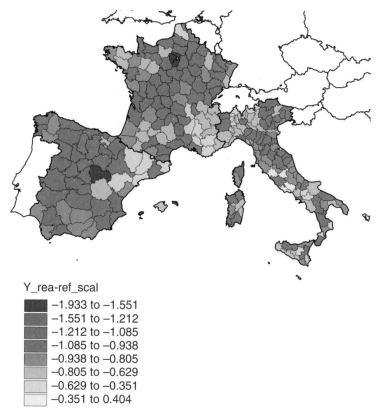

Y_rea-ref_scal
- ■ −1.933 to −1.551
- ■ −1.551 to −1.212
- ■ −1.212 to −1.085
- ■ −1.085 to −0.938
- ■ −0.938 to −0.805
- □ −0.805 to −0.629
- □ −0.629 to −0.351
- □ −0.351 to 0.404

*Map 6.3    Annual average GDP growth rates, 2005–2025: difference*
*between the defensive and the reference scenario*

## 6.4   CONCLUSIONS

This chapter has integrated the results of the MASST and the MAN models in order to build scenarios at sub-regional level. The assumptions at provincial level, given that the MAN-3 is a purely distributive model, had to follow a methodological logic different from the regional-level one developed earlier in Chapter 4. However, the economic logic is the same, and the scenarios developed in this chapter are faithful replications of the same conceptual scenarios as developed in Chapter 3, only at a much finer geographical disaggregation.

With NUTS-3 scenarios it would be possible to analyse policies more accurately with respect to NUTS-2 ones, given that the former are better able to capture territorial specificities. However, policy exercises, which will be the subject of Part IV, need a better qualitative/quantitative understanding of the processes ongoing at territorial level, also taking account of provincial specificities in aspects not represented in those variables which could be included in the econometric estimations. Therefore, before analysing the policy issues, Part III will focus on the Latin Arc, its structure and its territories. It will also provide a mechanism, labelled 'fine-tuning', to take account of provincial specificities which extend beyond the models.

# PART III

# The Latin Arc and the Barcelona case: strengths and weaknesses of the territorial structure

# 7. The Latin Arc

## Antonio Affuso and Ugo Fratesi

## 7.1 INTRODUCTION

In the previous chapters we have analysed the elements of territorial capital that play a role in explaining the differential growth rates of provinces with respect to their regions. As we have seen in Chapter 5, we are not able to capture all the effects. Some data, such as those describing the system of cultural elements and values which attribute sense and meaning to local practices and structures and define local identities, are not available, although they should be considered because they can boost the internal capacity to exploit local potentials. Hence, for exogenous reasons, the MAN-3 model is not able to take account of all the aspects of territorial capital which inspired its design.

As we shall see at the end of this chapter, it is possible to overcome this limitation by means of a simple procedure able to take into account provincial specificities and which is labelled 'fine-tuning'. This ought to provide a first response to the serious difficulty of considering all the variables affecting economic growth due to data problems and econometric issues which prevent the use of too many regressors at the same time.

No scenario exercise, however, is fruitful if it is unable to increase understanding of the mechanisms which work at territorial level and bring policy consequences. This also requires information which is more place specific than that obtainable from pure modelling results. Whence derives the need to apply the scenarios to a specific territory and the need to shed light on its geographic and economic structure.

The territory chosen for this analysis, which is preparatory for the policy chapters, is the Latin Arc network of provinces (ArcoLatino, 2010). This was selected because the book originates from an ESPON project. However, the Latin Arc network of provinces, as described in Section 7.3, is an area of great interest for putting scenarios to the test of territorial and policy consequences, since, as the rest of the chapter will show, its geographic and economic structure is highly differentiated and its role as a bridge between Europe and the Mediterranean articulates territorial needs which are often different from those of continental Europe.

No territorial scenario can be developed without considering the countries where those territories are located. Country effects, in fact, always constitute a very important part of regional growth, as evidenced in Chapter 4. Since all the Latin Arc provinces belong to three European countries – Spain, France and Italy – it is important to study the past performances of those countries and their structures, especially with regard to aspects underinvestigated by the MASST2 model. This will also help us confirm the reliability of results which appeared, at the time of the simulations (December 2009), rather counter-intuitive.

Accordingly, the chapter will follow a logic which goes from the general to the particular, first investigating the past growth and the structure of the three countries to which all provinces of the Latin Arc belong (Section 7.2). The origin and constitution of the Latin Arc network of provinces will then be illustrated, as well as the structure of its provinces, including their settlement structure and their features with respect to the countries to which they belong (Section 7.3). Finally, with the knowledge gathered from the previous two sections, the fine-tuning exercise will be possible and will be implemented in Section 7.4. The concluding section acts as an introduction to the following chapters, which will be devoted to policies.

## 7.2   LATIN ARC COUNTRIES: REINFORCING SCENARIO RESULTS

This section illustrates the growth performance and economic structure of the three European countries which comprise all the provinces of the Latin Arc. This has the ontological purpose of gaining knowledge on the context in which those provinces operate, but it also responds to the practical need to reinforce the results obtained by the MASST2 model at national level in Chapter 4.

In fact, at the time of the simulations (end of 2009), and even more substantially in the time span of the estimation time series, Spain appeared to consistently outperform the other two countries (OECD, 2008). It appeared counter-intuitive to see a similar trend of the other two countries, because its projected performance was lower than that of France and only higher than that of Italy, which is the European country whose growth rate has been most sluggish in the 2000s. However, the economic crisis which began in 2008 has brought to light structural weaknesses in many European countries, and especially those, such as Spain, whose growth was largely based on employment increases without sufficient productivity increases.

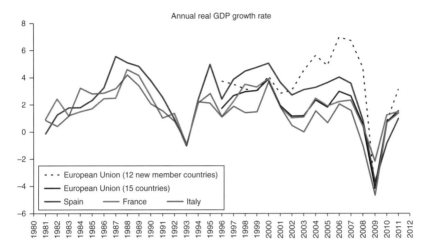

Annual real GDP growth rate

*Source:* Our elaborations on EUROSTAT data.

*Figure 7.1    GDP growth performance of Latin Arc countries in the past and short-run EUROSTAT projections (updated November 2009)*

Moreover, the construction and the financial sectors, which were very important for growth in the 1990s, proved more vulnerable than others to the crisis, so that specialization in them was a liability.

The past and the short-run EUROSTAT projections (Figure 7.1.) testify that the three Latin Arc countries have always been rather closely synchronized in their cycles, so that recessions tend to hit them similarly. In periods of growth, Spain has often outperformed both France and, especially, Italy (whose growth performance has been particularly disappointing), but in recent times Spain appears to have been hit by the crisis more strongly than France and is projected by official data to exit from the crisis more slowly than the other two countries. Figure 7.1 shows the real annual GDP growth rate from EUROSTAT statistics updated in November 2009. Obviously, only the data up to 2008 are actual data, whereas those for the following years are short-term projections.

Various explanations can be put forward for this change of trajectory. The first concerns the almost completed convergence process (in terms of per capita GDP) among the three countries, which cannot continue further without an overtaking. France started highest and has remained highest despite reducing its advantage over the rest of the EU. Spain, which started lowest, has been converging, but is now projected – by EUROSTAT – to suffer more than the other two countries from the crisis

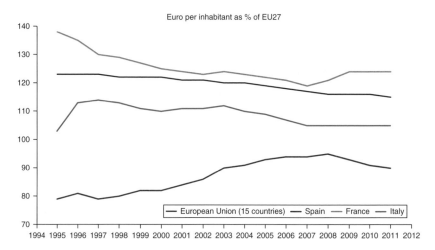

*Source:*    Our elaborations on EUROSTAT data.

*Figure 7.2*    *Convergence of the Latin Arc countries in terms of real GDP*
                *per capita (updated November 2009)*

(see Figure 7.2). Italy started below France and the EU15 average but
higher than the EU27 one and that of Spain, and despite its decline, still
remains in that position.

Real GDP, however, is not able to provide a full picture owing to the
different levels of prices among European countries. It is hence useful to
observe the same convergence in terms of purchasing power parity (PPP)
per inhabitant (Figure 7.3). In particular, it is possible to observe a very
poor performance by Italy, whose initial advantage has been eroded by
low growth and inflation, and a very good performance by Spain, whose
growth rates have been higher. As a result, in 2008 the disparities among
the three countries had almost disappeared with respect to the initial ones.
This means that Spain stands at around the level of France and above that
of Italy, but all three countries are now at a very similar level, which means
that convergence has substantially been accomplished.

Since Spain was so successful with respect to one of the other two
countries until 2007, it is interesting to consider in what respect its growth
model differs from those of France and Italy. Spain's model was based on
a high increase in employment and lower increases in labour productivity.
Moreover, the housing bubble appears to have characterized Spain much
more than France or Italy, as signalled by the fact that in 2008 the construction sector accounted for 9.22 per cent of GDP in Spain, compared
with 5.11 per cent for France and 5.36 per cent for Italy (Figure 7.4), and

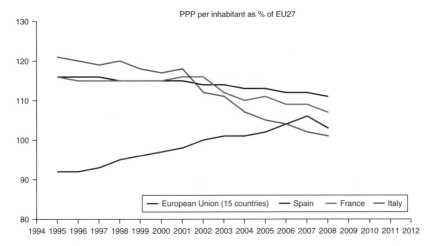

*Source:* Our elaborations on EUROSTAT data.

*Figure 7.3  Convergence of the Latin Arc countries in terms of purchasing power parity*

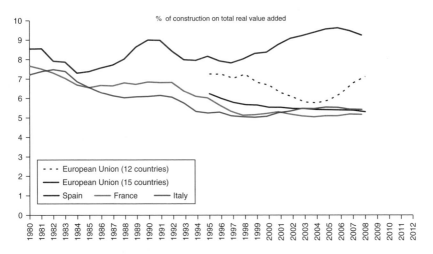

*Source:* Our elaborations on EUROSTAT data.

*Figure 7.4  Percentage of real value added generated by the construction sector*

*Table 7.1　FDI as a percentage of gross fixed capital formation*

|        |         | 1990–2000 (annual average) | 2006 | 2007 | 2008 |
|--------|---------|-----------|------|------|------|
| Spain  | Inward  | 10.9      | 9.9  | 6.3  | 13.9 |
|        | Outward | 11.5      | 26.6 | 21.5 | 16.4 |
| France | Inward  | 9.3       | 16.7 | 28.2 | 18.8 |
|        | Outward | 19.6      | 25.9 | 40.1 | 35.2 |
| Italy  | Inward  | 2.2       | 9.9  | 9.0  | 3.5  |
|        | Outward | 3.6       | 10.7 | 20.3 | 9.1  |

*Source:*　UNCTAD (2009).

by the fact that, in a period in which the construction sector lost importance for the rest of the EU15, including France and Italy, only in Spain did it increase its share.

Finally, there is an inversion in the pattern of foreign direct investment (FDI) (Table 7.1). As Spain has become richer and converged towards the rest of the EU, it has shifted from being an attractor of FDI to a net exporter of capital. As shown by data from the *World Investment Report* (UNCTAD, 2009), in the 1990–2000 period, Spain imported and exported about the same amount of capital, whereas France was a net outward investor and Italy had a very closed economy. In recent years, all three countries, but especially France and Spain, have been net exporters of capital, so that this difference between France and Spain has also disappeared. Doubts concerning the long-term sustainability of Spain's outstanding performance already existed in 2007, and they are more substantial today (for example, Torrero, 2009).

Figure 7.5 shows the dynamics of the labour markets in the three countries. They have a similar trend in the employment structure. Of particular interest is the decrease in the share of agriculture employment for all countries, as well as the steady reduction in manufacturing employment. In Spain the decrease in agriculture has been very marked, falling from a share on total employment of 7 to 4 per cent.

With regard to service employment, in France, where the share was already large, the growth has been lower than in Italy, and especially in Spain. In the last country, between 1999 and 2008 the share of service employment increased by 6 per cent, against a share growing by about 4 per cent in Italy and in France. This trend reveals the increased importance of the service sector in industrialized economies. These figures also aid understanding of the productive structures of the Latin Arc countries. France is

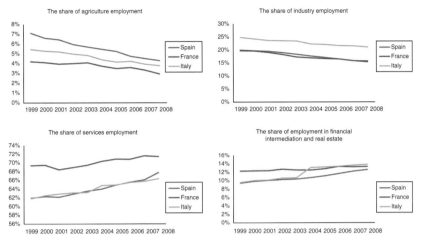

*Source:* Our elaboration on ESPON data.

*Figure 7.5  Employment in the Latin Arc countries*

clearly biased towards a service economy, whereas in Italy the manufacturing sector is still heavily present. In Spain the production structure has been changing rapidly due to strong economic development in recent years.

Analysis of the share of employment in financial intermediation and real estate shows that the service economy is mostly concentrated in financial services. A possible explanation for the step in the Italian curve, apart from probable changes in the data collection procedure, is that there was a strong increase in house prices in those years and a proliferation of real estate brokers, as well as a liberalization of the consumer credit market, which may also have contributed to Italy's performance.

As a final comparison between the patterns followed by the three Latin Arc countries, Figure 7.6 presents the annual behaviour of labour productivity. Interestingly, the analysis reveals that France has outperformed the others in the past two decades, although it already started at the highest level. The behaviours are explained by different factors in each country.

The French economy has grown by about 2 per cent annually over the past 10 years, which is slightly less than the best performing European countries. During this period, there has been strong growth in productivity in the manufacturing sector; but the trend in overall productivity has been less positive, reflecting in particular the weaker productivity growth in the service sector depending in part on the increased participation of low-skilled workers.

Exposure to international competition, by contrast, has helped improve productivity in manufacturing. In fact, European integration has contributed

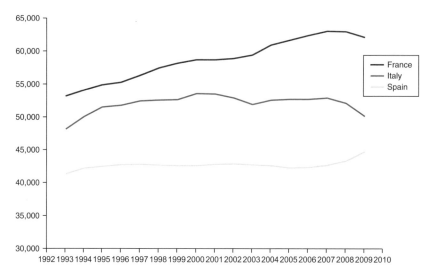

*Source:*  OECD.Stat.

*Figure 7.6    Labour productivity in Latin Arc countries*

to the openness of the French economy, and the presence of multinationals tends to be higher than in other countries of comparable size.

The development of productivity in the service sector has not benefited from international competition to the same extent, because France's international trade in services is much lower than that of manufactured goods, and because the presence of foreign affiliates in the service sector tends to be lower than in other countries (OECD, 2009a).

A decade of almost nil productivity growth and deterioration of competitiveness has left Italy behind the other countries in terms of GDP growth. Some of the causes of low productivity are rooted in bad or excessive regulation, public services and administration, and the legal system. Progress has been made in improving regulation, although the results have not been apparent in productivity growth (OECD, 2009b).

In Spain, productivity growth has also been sluggish and the very positive GDP performance has only been driven by a large increase in employment, including low-qualified jobs. In fact, barriers to competition are still significant, also in sectors producing intermediate goods and services, and they extend their negative impact on productivity throughout the economy. Particularly in sectors such as energy, telecommunications, transport and postal services, as well as other markets including savings banks and the retail trade, there is still room to increase productivity (OECD, 2009c).

A last aspect to be observed concerns the first effects of the crisis, which appear to be different among countries. In France the crisis has led to a halt in productivity growth, which has slightly decreased. In Italy, owing to automatic welfare mechanisms, employment levels have been maintained more than in other countries, and for this reason productivity has decreased to a greater extent. The effects on Spain of the beginning of the crisis is exactly the opposite: in a country with low productivity, the crisis has led to the shedding of a large number of unprotected jobs and, therefore, Spain's productivity has even increased.

## 7.3   THE LATIN ARC NETWORK

### 7.3.1   The Latin Arc Network: An Introduction

The Latin Arc is a network of cooperation among local institutions in which integrated actions in different policy fields can improve economic and social cohesion in member regions. As pointed out in the European Territorial Strategy, cooperation is essential to correct regional imbalances. Moreover, the goal is to make the Latin Arc members more competitive and socially integrated by improving the conservation of the natural and cultural environment, identities and traditions.

This association was founded in 1999 and officially constituted as an association in 2002 in Montpellier. The reasons for creation of the Latin Arc network consist in the need to respond to the problems of local institutions, which are often unknown and underestimated at both European and national and regional levels.

Before the formal constitution of the Latin Arc network, there were numerous forms of transboundary cooperation among the Mediterranean provinces of Italy, France and Spain. However, in some cases, this cooperation among neighbouring regions of countries was insufficient to meet more important challenges successfully. Therefore, it was decided to establish a partnership extending beyond national borders. The Conseil Général des Alpes-Maritimes proposed the creation of the Latin Arc network, as a response to these challenges and as an instrument to develop and consolidate more stable cooperation dynamics with a greater impact than that of existing initiatives.

After a first meeting in Marseilles, in which 32 administrations participated, the First General Assembly was held (Barcelona, June 2001). On that occasion, 37 administrations signed the Joint Declaration, the network's first political positioning and reference document. Thereafter, the Latin Arc's efforts focused on gaining legal status, on establishing a stable common structure, and on securing the territorial continuity of the western Mediterranean area.

In June 2002, at the Latin Arc constitutive General Assembly in Montpellier, the association's founding statutes were signed by 56 administrations. At this Assembly, the president of the Diputació de Barcelona was elected first president of the association, while the other administrative board members were also appointed and a Permanent Secretariat was constituted. This Permanent Secretariat was divided into a Strategic Secretariat coordinated by Conseil Général de l'Hérault, a Technical Secretariat coordinated by Provincia di Roma, and three territorial secretariats coordinated by the Diputación de Sevilla, the Provincia di Genova and the Conseil Général de l'Hérault.

At the General Assembly in Barcelona (November 2004) the administrative board was renewed and a new presidency, the Conseil Général de l'Hérault, was elected. A new Permanent Secretariat, coordinated by the Diputació de Barcelona, was also constituted. In January 2007, on the occasion of the General Assembly in Nuoro, a new mandate under the presidency of the Province of Torino began. The network has succeeded in giving visibility to the territory in Europe and has been recognized as an area of community development.

As stated above, one of the objectives of the Latin Arc network is to build an area of political cooperation among second-level administrations (NUTS-3 level). The Latin Arc is a platform for administrations wishing to enhance their ability to interact and achieve jointly defined objectives. Moreover, Latin Arc members can define joint initiatives (communication, political and pilot projects) necessary for the development of this Euro-territory and with a major impact.

The specific goals of the Latin Arc network are:

- definition of an integrated development and planning strategy for the Latin Arc area, including and mobilizing socioeconomic actors from the bottom to the top;
- establishment of a regular, dynamic and flexible agreement focused on the most important fields of regional development;
- cooperation among provinces to launch common projects and initiatives;
- defence of regional interests and needs in front of the EU and national institutions; and
- creation of a space of cooperation with the South Mediterranean countries.

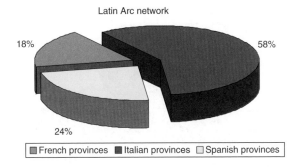

Latin Arc network

18%   24%   58%

☐ French provinces  ■ Italian provinces  ☐ Spanish provinces

*Source:*  ArcoLatino (2010).

*Figure 7.7   Latin Arc network provinces*

The Latin Arc network currently has 101 active members (59 Italian, 24 Spanish and 18 French) (see Figure 7.7).

In the broadest geographical sense, the Latin Arc is a large area with more than 70 million inhabitants in the territories of four EU member states: Spain, France, Italy and Portugal. The Latin Arc network includes, however, only Spanish and Italian provinces and the French departments in the western Mediterranean. It covers a territory that extends from Andalucia to Sicily (Map 7.1).

Describing the Latin Arc administratively is not sufficient to build policies in this area; knowledge on its economic structure is also necessary. In order to provide a description of the economy of the Latin Arc network, the next subsection will present the main features of those provinces compared with the others of their respective countries and of the EU. The aim of Section 7.3.2 is therefore to present and summarize certain characteristics of the provinces of the Latin Arc network. This will provide the framework in which we will fine-tune our econometric results, which will then introduce the policies described in the next chapters.

Following the literature, we consider it is necessary to improve our analysis by using elements of territorial capital able to boost the internal capacity to exploit local potentials, and which are not contained in our MAN model because of a lack of homogeneous data on the provinces of the three countries. In our opinion, the most important elements are transport infrastructure endowment, measured also in terms of *potential accessibility,* and *human capital.*

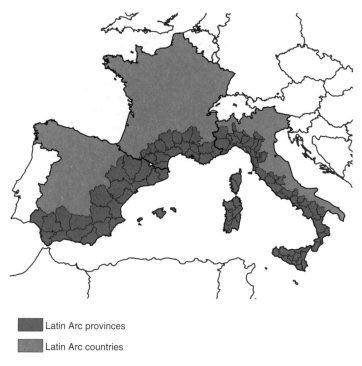

■ Latin Arc provinces

■ Latin Arc countries

*Source:*  ArcoLatino (2010).

*Map 7.1    Latin Arc network provinces and countries*

### 7.3.2    The Economic Structure of the Provinces of the Latin Arc Network

In order to build the framework for the fine-tuning and to describe the territorial specificities of the provinces in the Latin Arc network – specificities
at the basis of their economic performance – an analysis of the settlement
structure of provinces is important and, analogously to what was done for
countries in Section 7.2, so too is a description of their specialization in the
construction sector, given its role in the past economic crisis. The analysis
first involves all provinces of the three countries, which are then compared
with provinces in the Latin Arc network.

The data presented in Table 7.2 illustrate differences between Italy
and the other two countries, Spain and France, with particular regard to
the 'rural' provinces.[1] In the last two countries, 37 per cent of provinces

[1]  Rural provinces are defined in Table 5.1.

*Table 7.2    Share of employment by settlement structure and specialization in construction at NUTS-3 level (%)*

|  | Agglomerated provinces | Urban provinces | Rural provinces | Provinces specialized in construction |
|---|---|---|---|---|
| *Latin Arc provinces* | | | | |
| France | 13.0 | 50.0 | 37.0 | 36.0 |
| Italy | 31.8 | 46.7 | 21.5 | 46.7 |
| Spain | 20.3 | 42.4 | 37.3 | 42.4 |
| *Latin Arc network* | | | | |
| France | 11.1 | 55.6 | 33.3 | 55.6 |
| Italy | 25.4 | 50.8 | 23.7 | 55.9 |
| Spain | 20.8 | 45.8 | 33.3 | 41.7 |

*Source:*   EUROSTAT.

are rural, while only 21 per cent are in Italy. This indicates that Italy has a settlement structure shifted more towards urban and agglomerated provinces, that is, those with higher population densities or large cities. Indeed, 79 per cent of Italian provinces belong to these two categories, compared with 62 per cent of Spanish provinces and the 63 per cent of French ones.

Some interesting facts also emerge from analysis of the percentages of provinces specialized in construction. We measure the specialization using the ratio between employees in construction and total employment. Provinces with a ratio above the country average are specialized. Surprisingly, Italy shows a percentage of 'construction sector' specialized provinces higher than that of Spain. This result is driven by the Italian southern provinces, where construction is the main economic sector of activity.

It emerges from comparing these results that provinces belonging to the Latin Arc network are more 'urban' than the average of all three countries. The consequence is that they are also more specialized in construction, given that in urban areas the construction sector, especially with reference to infrastructure and public and private housing, is of great importance. The sole exception is Spain, where provinces in the Latin Arc network are slightly less specialized in construction than the country average: 41.7 against 42.4 per cent.

According to the ideas that the stock of public capital matters in explaining the evolution of productivity, and that basic infrastructure (mainly in transport, water and energy) shows the closest relationship to productivity (Aschauer, 1989), in light of the above findings on productivity

*Table 7.3    Transport infrastructure endowment of provinces*

|  | Average km of road on area | Average km of rail on area |
|---|---|---|
| *Latin Arc network* | | |
| France | 0.094 | 0.045 |
| Italy | 0.062 | 0.052 |
| Spain | 0.131 | 0.020 |
| *Latin Arc provinces* | | |
| France | 0.161 | 0.075 |
| Italy | 0.074 | 0.056 |
| Spain | 0.134 | 0.022 |

*Source:*  ESPON database.

growth, an analysis of transport endowment infrastructure is of interest. Nevertheless, infrastructures have different effects on economic growth in different countries.

For example, Forni and Paba (2000) show that transport infrastructure does not affect growth in Italy, whereas it plays an important role in Spain. Indeed, as we saw in Chapter 5, Holl (2004) finds that in the context of a country such as Spain, access to road transport infrastructure plays an important role in manufacturing plant location, and that motorways affect the spatial distribution of new manufacturing establishments by increasing the attractiveness of areas close to the new infrastructure.

Table 7.3. sets out the different infrastructure densities among provinces in the Latin Arc network. The result achieved by Spain in road infrastructure is immediately apparent. On average, Spanish provinces have 0.131 km of road per sq. km, while Italy has 0.062 and France 0.094. Not surprisingly, all countries have a more capillary-type road network than the rail network. What is interesting for our analysis is that in all countries the provinces belonging to the network have an infrastructure density below the country average.

In Table 7.4. the infrastructure density of provinces is analysed on the basis of their settlement structure. With regard to the road infrastructure, in all three countries the agglomerated provinces are the best endowed, while the rural provinces are the least so. This is not surprising, given the higher population density that characterizes agglomerated regions. With regard to the provinces in the Latin Arc network, the only ones registering a density above the average are the agglomerated Italian provinces and the Spanish urban provinces, which confirms that,

*Table 7.4* *Transport infrastructure endowment of provinces by settlement structure*

|  | Average km of road on area | | | Average km of rail on area | | |
|---|---|---|---|---|---|---|
|  | Agglo-merated | Urban | Rural | Agglo-merated | Urban | Rural |
| French provinces | 0.450 | 0.138 | 0.091 | 0.198 | 0.063 | 0.048 |
| French provinces in the Latin Arc network | 0.107 | 0.106 | 0.068 | 0.080 | 0.047 | 0.031 |
| Italian provinces | 0.102 | 0.074 | 0.029 | 0.083 | 0.046 | 0.038 |
| Italian provinces in the Latin Arc network | 0.109 | 0.060 | 0.016 | 0.087 | 0.047 | 0.030 |
| Spanish provinces | 0.235 | 0.126 | 0.087 | 0.035 | 0.022 | 0.016 |
| Spanish provinces in the Latin Arc network | 0.167 | 0.148 | 0.085 | 0.039 | 0.017 | 0.011 |

*Source:* ESPON database.

in general, the Latin Arc provinces are below the average. The same applies if the endowment of rail infrastructure is analysed, with the exception of Italy: indeed, owing to its morphology, Italy's rail network is mainly located in coastal provinces, many of which belong to the Latin Arc.

A concept directly linked with the transport infrastructure is that of 'accessibility'. Indeed, the task of transport infrastructure is to enable spatial interaction. In the context of spatial development, the quality of transport infrastructure in terms of capacity, connectivity and travel speeds, determines the competitive advantage of an area relative to other locations. Indicators of accessibility measure the benefits deriving to households and firms in an area from the existence and use of the transport infrastructure relevant to that area (Wegener et al., 2002).

In ESPON 1.2.1, a broad range of indicators describing the transport system were developed, among them different accessibility indicators such as travel time, daily accessibility and potential accessibility. In our analysis on the Latin Arc provinces we specifically used the potential accessibility indicators of the ESPON 1.2.1 project, which reflect the situation in the year 2001.

Considering that 100 is the average in European countries, it follows from Table 7.5 that only French and Italian agglomerated provinces in the Latin Arc network boast an index higher than 100. This is especially interesting because we have seen that Spanish agglomerated provinces were those with the highest road density, but in this case they have the lowest index, which shows that local roads are normally not correlated with longer-range networks. Finally, confirming the previous results, it is also evident that, with rare exceptions, all provinces in the network have an average index of potential accessibility lower than that of all provinces in each country.

Human capital is considered in the most recent literature as both a result of development and a precondition for it: a higher initial level of human capital induces a higher growth rate, and in its turn economic growth reinforces human capital accumulation. Various empirical works have shown that human capital explains growth differentials among countries, once the effects of the level of per capita income on human capital have been offset.

Human capital affects growth, increasing the level and the rate of growth of productivity, and it does so directly and indirectly: directly because skilled labour is more productive, and indirectly because the endowment of human capital affects the capacity and the speed of absorption of technical innovations (Nelson and Phelps, 1966; Aghion and Cohen, 2004).

The seminal paper on human capital in the endogenous theory of growth is Lucas (1988), where educated labour is the production factor entering the extended concept of capital with constant marginal productivity; investment in education then sustains human capital accumulation and economic growth. An important empirical finding supporting this theoretical hypothesis is that by Barro (2001), who finds that an additional year of schooling raises the growth rate by 0.44 per year.

With this in mind, we now analyse the human capital endowment of the provinces of the Latin Arc network. Table 7.6 shows that, on average, French provinces have a higher share of people with tertiary education than the other two countries. Italian provinces have the lowest percentage of professionals in the population, while Spain has the highest percentage. As expected, because human capital tends to concentrate in cities,

*Table 7.5   Potential accessibility indicators*

| | Potential accessibility air | Potential accessibility rail | Potential accessibility road | Potential accessibility multimodal |
|---|---|---|---|---|
| | Agglomerated | | | |
| French provinces | 124.00 | 147.46 | 131.15 | 124.54 |
| French provinces in the Latin Arc network | 122.50 | 100.50 | 89.00 | 118.50 |
| Italian provinces | 109.79 | 97.29 | 106.76 | 108.68 |
| Italian provinces in the Latin Arc network | 109.27 | 89.93 | 100.60 | 108.07 |
| Spanish provinces | 73.17 | 30.83 | 33.17 | 68.92 |
| Spanish provinces in the Latin Arc network | 96.60 | 39.40 | 42.60 | 90.80 |
| | Urban | | | |
| French provinces | 85.76 | 120.38 | 116.24 | 92.36 |
| French provinces in the Latin Arc network | 87.10 | 88.40 | 80.30 | 87.90 |
| Italian provinces | 88.32 | 77.00 | 86.58 | 87.58 |
| Italian provinces in the Latin Arc network | 88.73 | 66.23 | 74.03 | 86.67 |
| Spanish provinces | 59.36 | 30.44 | 33.48 | 56.92 |
| Spanish provinces in the Latin Arc network | 63.18 | 30.27 | 32.00 | 60.27 |
| | Rural | | | |
| French provinces | 58.05 | 86.57 | 86.92 | 64.54 |
| French provinces in the Latin Arc network | 63.33 | 63.00 | 71.50 | 64.00 |
| Italian provinces | 59.43 | 47.04 | 58.52 | 58.96 |
| Italian provinces in the Latin Arc network | 48.64 | 29.43 | 36.00 | 47.36 |
| Spanish provinces | 38.14 | 25.50 | 29.59 | 37.36 |
| Spanish provinces in the Latin Arc network | 35.75 | 24.75 | 28.38 | 34.75 |

*Source:*   ESPON database.

*Table 7.6    Share of human capital endowment of provinces by settlement structure (%)*

| | People with tertiary education over population | | | Professional jobs over population | | |
|---|---|---|---|---|---|---|
| | Agglo-merated | Urban | Rural | Agglo-merated | Urban | Rural |
| French provinces | 15.8 | 11.6 | 9.3 | 5.0 | 3.3 | 2.9 |
| French provinces in the Latin Arc network | 15.2 | 12.4 | 10.8 | 4.1 | 3.4 | 2.9 |
| Italian provinces | 6.7 | 6.3 | 6.1 | 3.4 | 3.2 | 3.1 |
| Italian provinces in the Latin Arc network | 7.0 | 6.2 | 5.8 | 3.5 | 3.1 | 3.0 |
| Spanish provinces | 5.9 | 4.8 | 3.8 | 4.9 | 4.3 | 3.9 |
| Spanish provinces in the Latin Arc network | 5.7 | 3.9 | 3.6 | 4.8 | 3.8 | 3.8 |

*Source:* EUROSTAT-ISCED 5–6 for tertiary education and EUROSTAT-ISCO 2 for professional jobs.

agglomerated regions have higher values with respect to urban ones and, even more so, rural ones.

Looking at the Latin Arc network, it seems that its endowment of human capital is almost in line with the three countries, since the values are very similar. With regard to national specificities, French urban and rural provinces in the Latin Arc network present above-average shares, both of people with a tertiary education and of those with a professional job. The contrary holds for agglomerated provinces. In Italy, agglomerated provinces are the only ones with values above the average of all national provinces, whereas in Spain the provinces of the Latin Arc network are all underendowed.

Linked with the presence of human capital is the degree of innovation, which is of great importance for the definition of local competitiveness. Given the lack of data on knowledge creation and innovation activities at NUTS-3 level, human capital can be a relatively good proxy for innovation processes. All the data presented thus far constitute the basis for the fine-tuning developed in the next section.

## 7.4 FINE-TUNING ON THE LATIN ARC PROVINCES

The MAN-3 model cannot fully explain differential growth rates. In fact, as we have seen in the previous sections, the geographic and economic structure of the Latin Arc is highly differentiated internally. To take account of this, other elements have been identified, which are not included in the regression model but which can help explain differential growth rates between provinces in the same region. Data on *human capital, accessibility*, and *tourism* performance are considered for this purpose.

Provinces are ranked into five classes of endowment with these elements – high, high–medium, medium, low–medium and low – on the basis of data analysed in detail in Section 7.2. In particular, seven available indicators for accessibility, namely the length of road (km) per sq. km, the length of railway (km) per sq. km, the time to the nearest motorway access by car from the capital or centroid representative of the NUTS-3, potential accessibility by air, potential accessibility by rail, potential accessibility by road, and potential multimodal accessibility. Two indicators are used for human capital, namely the percentage of the population with tertiary education, and the percentage of professional jobs in the active population; and one indicator is used for tourism performance, namely the growth rate of the total number of establishments, bedrooms and beds between 1997 and 2006.

All provinces are first ranked according to each indicator individually. Then a ranking for each of the three elements (human capital, accessibility and tourism performance) is built by aggregating them. Finally the rankings in the three elements are combined into an overall one by a simple sum of the three rankings. The main advantage of this aggregative procedure is its simplicity, and it is made possible by the fact that there is little correlation between the three indicators and the interest here is only to identify those provinces with extreme rankings. In this way it is possible to identify provinces in the Latin Arc network with the highest endowments of these three elements of territorial competitiveness.

This is not sufficient to decide to amend the MAN-3 results, because regions with high or low endowments of those factors could be correctly estimated in any case because of their high or low endowments of other factors. For this reason, provincial growth rates not explained by the model must be considered, which can be done by using the *residuals* of the regression in Chapter 5. Once provinces have been ranked using the residuals, those provinces that our MAN-3 regression has overestimated to a greater extent are extracted from the ranking; these are the provinces with positive residuals higher than 1. Likewise extracted are those provinces

*Table 7.7　　Adjusted provinces*

| (a) Overestimated provinces | | | (b) Underestimated provinces | | |
|---|---|---|---|---|---|
| NUTS-3 | Latin Arc provinces | Final weighted ranking | NUTS-3 | Latin Arc provinces | Final weighted ranking |
| ITG15 | Caltanissetta | 15.33 | ITD54 | Modena | −4.68 |
| ITE1A | Grosseto | 13.72 | ITG13 | Messina | −5.33 |
| ITC16 | Cuneo | 12.71 | ES613 | Córdoba | −5.53 |
| ITE41 | Viterbo | 9.28 | ITF21 | Isernia | −6.04 |
| ITG18 | Ragusa | 8.82 | ITD52 | Parma | −6.42 |
| ES521 | Alicante | 8.80 | ITC17 | Asti | −6.90 |
| ITC4B | Mantova | 7.88 | ITC18 | Alessandria | −8.22 |
| | | | ES241 | Huesca | −11.33 |
| | | | ITC31 | Imperia | −15.34 |

that are underestimated to a greater extent, that is, those with negative residuals lower than −1.

Finally, the overall ranking of territorial elements is combined with the residuals of provinces by identifying those provinces which have been highly underestimated but have high endowments of those structural elements which could not be included in the estimation model (Table 7.7b).[2] Similarly identified are those provinces which have been highly overestimated and which have low endowments of structural elements (Table 7.7a).[3]

As a consequence of the exercise, it is possible to observe in Map 7.2 the results of the baseline scenario of MAN-3 with two different grids evidencing the 'adjusted' provinces: seven overestimated and nine underestimated provinces. This allows us to state that the actual growth rates in the scenario should be higher for the underestimated and lower for the overestimated provinces with respect to the growth rates presented in Chapter 6, or, in other words, that the MAN-3 projected growth rate should be considered as the minimum one for underestimated provinces and the maximum one for overestimated ones.

This analysis also shows that Italian provinces are more present among those with problems of mis-estimation, signalling that our econometric model is able to explain France and Spain more than Italy. A possible reason for this behaviour resides in the heterogeneous economic

---

[2]　Provinces with negative residuals lower than −1 and ranked as high, high–medium, and medium.

[3]　Provinces ranked as low, low–medium, and medium and positive residuals higher than 1.

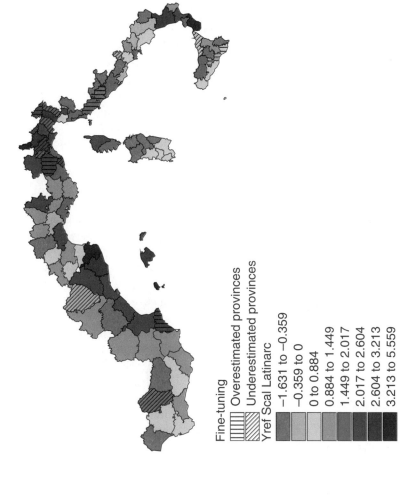

Fine-tuning

▥ Overestimated provinces
▨ Underestimated provinces
▨ Yref Scal Latinarc

▨ −1.631 to −0.359
▨ −0.359 to 0
▨ 0 to 0.884
▨ 0.884 to 1.449
▨ 1.449 to 2.017
▨ 2.017 to 2.604
▨ 2.604 to 3.213
▨ 3.213 to 5.559

*Map 7.2    Annual average GDP growth rate, 2005–2025; fine-tuning of the reference scenario*

structure of Italian provinces characterized by deep diversity between macro-regions, such as North-East versus North-West or North versus Mezzogiorno, but also by a different distribution of territorial capital elements among provinces.

## 7.5   CONCLUSIONS

This chapter has presented the area which will be the object of the policy studies conducted in the following chapters. This area is known as the 'Latin Arc network', which is an organization of provinces belonging to three European countries: France, Italy and Spain.

The growth performances of these three countries have been different in the past, more in terms of economic model than in performance, although Spain has outperformed the other two, and France has outperformed Italy. However, the Spanish growth model appears to be less sustainable, as the MASST model (Chapter 4) and the data on the impact of the economic crisis appear to show.

The Latin Arc network has also been analysed at a finer territorial scale, that is, NUTS-3, because Chapter 5 showed that we are not able to capture the entire complexity of the Latin Arc territories, which have been presented here as a heterogeneous network composed of regions with effects which depend on the country to which they belong (such as the most important endowment of human capital in French provinces, or the higher specialization in construction for Spanish ones) and other effects which depend on belonging to the Latin Arc (such as the lower degree of infrastructure endowment).

Study of the Latin Arc network territory has made it possible to fine-tune the econometric results of Chapters 5 and 6 by considering more elements of territorial capital than those that could be included in the MAN-3 estimations. On the basis of the statistical analysis conducted in this chapter, it has hence been possible to fine-tune the results of the MAN-3 econometric model, considering them as minimum values for some underestimated provinces and maximum ones for other overestimated ones.

This calls for an even more territorially detailed level when dealing with policies to enhance the performance of regions in the three scenarios. For this reason, the next chapter will conduct a detailed analysis of the structure and performance of one important province of the Latin Arc, that is, the Diputació de Barcelona, in order to open the field for detailed and territorially aware policies.

# 8. The province of Barcelona

## Rafael Boix, Joan Trullén and Vittorio Galletto

## 8.1 BASIC FACTS AND MACROECONOMIC PERFORMANCE

The province of Barcelona is one of the four provinces (NUTS-3) that comprise Catalonia, located on the Mediterranean coast of Spain. Currently, in 2010, it has a population of 5.5 million inhabitants, encompasses an area of 7,700 km$^2$ and a population density of 715 hab/km$^2$.

Barcelona has a productive model characterized by the importance of its manufacturing base, its openness to foreign markets, and the central role of its small and medium-sized firms. One explanation for Barcelona's economic success lies in its agglomeration economies. To put this more precisely, the success of the province is due in the first place to its external economies of localization linked to both traditional and new industries, in the second place, to its urbanization economies generated by the scale of the metropolitan diversity, and finally to network economies derived from the existence of a network of cities generating synergies.

### 8.1.1 Population

The population of Barcelona has stabilized during the 1990s to about 4.6 million inhabitants. Between 2000 and 2010, the population rose to 5.5 million, with a 16 per cent accumulated growth rate. The arrival of foreign immigrants accounts for this population growth. The foreign-born population in the province rose from 150,000 in 2000 (3.2 per cent of the population in the province) to 690,000 in 2010 (14 per cent of the population) with an accumulated growth rate of 560 per cent. This attractiveness was due to the existence of a dynamic labour market offering a large number of low-qualified jobs.

The labour market is characterized in two different ways: a core of workers with permanent contract and high cost redundancy payment on the one hand and a rising number of young people and new foreign-born residents with insecure contracts and low cost redundancy pay on the other.

Despite the economic crisis, the population of the province has continued to grow more than 1 per cent annual average since 2007 due to immigration, which has provided more than 80 per cent of this growth.

### 8.1.2   Gross Domestic Product

GDP in 2010 is €150.000 million and the harmonized GDP per habitant in purchasing power parity (PPP) was €27,000, about 21 per cent above the EU27 and 13 per cent above EU15 average (Table 8.1) (source: IDESCAT and INE). The evolution of production (GDP) shows several different stages over the last 25 years: fast growth between 1986 and 1992, a severe recession between 1993 and 1994, recovery and intense growth between 1995 and 2007, and again a severe recession from the third trimester of 2007.

In the 1995–2007 period, the growth of GDP and gross added value increased about 3.5 per cent (annual average) at real prices. Services grew 3.9 per cent (annual average), manufacturing at 2 per cent and agriculture at 2.7 per cent. The largest growth rate belonged to construction with 4.9 per cent annual average. Although production increased in every sector, there was a change in sector weightings. Services rose from 63.5 to 67 per cent and construction from 5.7 to 8.8 per cent. On the other hand, manufacturing (including energy) fell from 30 to 24 per cent in terms of production, and agriculture from 0.7 to 0.6 per cent.

GDP rose until the second trimester of 2008, when the growth became negative. Until the second trimester of 2010 the growth rate was about −2.5 per cent annual average, and in the second trimester of 2010 became positive once more – despite limited growth. There was also a significant change in sector weightings, where the manufacturing share fell to 20.5 per cent and construction to 7.5 per cent, and services rose to 72 per cent of the production.

The EUROSTAT series allows us to compare the production of the province of Barcelona with the rest of the EU27 from 1995 (first year available in the homogeneous series). Thus, in 1995 the GDP per capita of the province was €13,900 (95 per cent of the EU27) whereas in 2007 it increased to €27,600 (110 per cent of the EU27 average) (Table 8.1). As a consequence, there was an intense process of convergence in GDP per capita of about 15 per cent (about 1 per cent every year). In fact, when the data are expressed in PPP, the figure rises to 130 per cent EU27 average.

### 8.1.3   Employment and Unemployment

Employment growth in the province of Barcelona between 1986 and 2007 has been very impressive: from 1,852,000 to 2,775,000 jobs, that is,

Table 8.1   GDP at current market prices at NUTS-3 level: province of Barcelona

| | 1995 | 2000 | 2005 | 2006 | 2007 | Growth 1995–2007, units | Growth 1995–2007, % |
|---|---|---|---|---|---|---|---|
| *Euros per inhabitant* | | | | | | | |
| EU27 | 14,700 | 19,100 | 22,500 | 23,600 | 24,900 | 10,300 | 70.1 |
| EU15 | 18,085 | 23,186 | 26,761 | 27,970 | 29,239 | 11,200 | 61.9 |
| Spain | 11,600 | 15,700 | 20,900 | 22,300 | 23,500 | 11,900 | 102.6 |
| Catalunya | 14,100 | 19,100 | 24,800 | 26,300 | 27,500 | 13,400 | 95.0 |
| Barcelona | 13,900 | 18,900 | 24,800 | 26,300 | 27,600 | 13,700 | 98.6 |
| *Millions of euros (from 1.1.1999)/millions of ECU (up to 31.12.1998)* | | | | | | | |
| EU27 | 7,012,911 | 9,201,967 | 11,061,982 | 11,671,360 | 12,362,787 | 5,377,767 | 76.6 |
| EU15 | 6,740,683 | 8,763,924 | 10,396,375 | 10,924,332 | 11,493,554 | 4,781,638 | 70.9 |
| Spain | 456,495 | 630,263 | 908,792 | 982,303 | 1,052,730 | 596,235 | 130.6 |
| Catalunya | 86,084 | 119,225 | 170,109 | 184,035 | 197,254 | 111,170 | 129.1 |
| Barcelona | 64,994 | 89,838 | 127,021 | 136,880 | 146,469 | 81,475 | 125.4 |
| Barcelona over EU27 | 0.93% | 0.98% | 1.15% | 1.17% | 1.18% | 0.26% | 27.6 |

*Source:*   Elaborations on EUROSTAT.

*Table 8.2*   *Employment by sector, Barcelona province, 1996–2007 (per 1,000 employees)*

|  | 1995 | 2000 | 2005 | 2006 (P) | 2007 (P) | Growth 1995–2007 | Growth 1995–2007, 1995=100 |
|---|---|---|---|---|---|---|---|
| Agriculture | 23 | 29 | 31 | 34 | 28 | 5 | 122 |
| Energy | 12 | 12 | 13 | 13 | 14 | 2 | 117 |
| Manufacturing | 486 | 620 | 612 | 602 | 588 | 102 | 121 |
| Construction | 126 | 194 | 229 | 253 | 265 | 139 | 210 |
| Services | 1,206 | 1,446 | 1,775 | 1,864 | 1,950 | 744 | 162 |
| Total employment | 1,852 | 2,300 | 2,659 | 2,766 | 2,845 | 993 | 154 |

*Note:*   (P) Provisional.

*Sources:*   CRE (Contabilidad Regional de España: Regional Accounts of Spain); and INE (Instituto Nacional de Estadística: National Statistics Institute of Spain).

a 50 per cent accumulated growth rate over 20 years. It might be said to be one of the strongest increments in employment in recent EU history. Employment growth has been continuous, with the exception of 1993–94 and since 2007 (Table 8.2). However, the 2007 crisis has demonstrated a weakness in part of the model. In fact, an important part of this growth was due to low-qualified jobs in construction and services. In addition, more than 30 per cent of the jobs were unstable. The growth rate of employment became negative from the end of 2007 to the first trimester of 2010, with a negative annual growth rate above 4 per cent. Since the second trimester of 2010 the province is again generating employment at rates of more than 1 per cent.

Regarding the structure of employment by sector, two main trends can be observed. First, in the 1995–2007 period relative growth has been positive in all sectors: 21 per cent in manufacturing, 110 per cent in construction and 62 per cent in services. Second, the total growth was particularly strong in the services sector. This means that, contrary to most analysts' opinion, the growth of the province was not led by the construction sector that created 139,000 new jobs, but instead by the tertiary sector (744,000 new jobs) and by manufacturing (102,000 new jobs).

The crisis has deeply affected employment in manufacturing and construction although in different ways. Manufacturing has lost 150,000 jobs and contributed to 49 per cent of the total job loss, due largely to a fall in external (foreign) and Spanish demand. The construction sector has lost

*Table 8.3    Evolution of employment during the crisis (Index 2008/1st trimester = 100), Barcelona province*

| Year | Trimester | Total | Agri-culture | Manu-facturing and energy | Con-struction | Services |
|------|-----------|-------|--------|-----------|-----------|----------|
| 2008 | 1st | 100 | 100 | 100 | 100 | 100 |
| 2008 | 2nd | 100 | 95.6 | 96.2 | 97.5 | 101.8 |
| 2008 | 3rd | 97.3 | 78.0 | 92.0 | 91.6 | 100.4 |
| 2008 | 4th | 94.8 | 82.0 | 86.1 | 89.2 | 98.9 |
| 2009 | 1st | 89.9 | 63.4 | 82.4 | 82.3 | 94.1 |
| 2009 | 2nd | 87.8 | 66.3 | 77.0 | 79.5 | 93.3 |
| 2009 | 3rd | 88.2 | 71.7 | 75.2 | 76.2 | 95.0 |
| 2009 | 4th | 87.9 | 74.1 | 76.2 | 74.1 | 94.5 |
| 2010 | 1st | 86.9 | 85.9 | 75.8 | 74.7 | 92.9 |
| 2010 | 2nd | 87.5 | 96.6 | 75.7 | 69.7 | 94.5 |
| 2010 | 3rd | 88.2 | 99.0 | 74.9 | 67.1 | 96.3 |

*Source:*   Elaborations on INE.

more than 90,000 employees, contributed about 30 per cent to the total job loss, and shows a negative growth rate of 33 per cent, eight points higher than those of the manufacturing sector (Table 8.3). On the other hand, the service sector has been less affected by the crisis as it has lost only 4 per cent of the jobs in the province, even if this means 64,000 jobs, and contributed to 21 per cent of the total job loss.

Although to a lesser extent than the Spanish economy, part of the growth model of Barcelona's economy was based on low-qualified employment in construction and in some service activities, comprising a considerable number of immigrants, and therefore sensitive to the effects of the crisis. Furthermore, the manufacturing export base of the province was very focused on external markets so that the fall in demand during 2008 and 2009 also affected manufacturing sectors. Job loss (10.5 per cent in three years) and the continuous growth of the active population caused the unemployment rate to grow from 6.5 per cent in 2007 to 17.8 per cent in 2010.

### 8.1.4    Productivity

Despite the impressive increase in production in the 1995–2007 period, the growth rate of employment was quite similar to that of GDP, so productivity growth has been low. It was negative between 1997 and 2001, barely positive from 2002 to 2005, and close to zero in 2006–07. Since the growth rate of production can be explained as the sum of the growth rate of employment plus the growth rate of productivity, these data mean that almost the whole increase in production has been explained by the growth of employment, particularly by the fast growth in sectors where productivity tends to rise slowly (construction and services). This low productivity growth reflects production with a relatively low use of human and financial capital. Manufacturing was the only sector boosting the growth of productivity in the economy of Barcelona (and in Spain as a whole). The growth of productivity in this sector has been important since the year 2000, and particularly between 2004 and 2007. After 2007, the fall in production was quite mild whereas job loss was high, producing an increase in productivity.

### 8.1.5    Firm Size

One of the distinctive features of the economy of Barcelona is that the average size of firms and establishments is small, approximately 4.9 employees/unit. Research has shown that this size is similar to industrial economies such as Japan and European Mediterranean countries, whereas the rest of the EU and the USA tend to be two or three times larger than the average size. The average firm size in the EU is about six employees per productive unit (EUROSTAT Structural Business Statistics).

Approximately 97 per cent of firms have fewer than 50 employees, whereas medium-sized firms in their entirety constitute 2.3 per cent and large firms 0.41 per cent. The province of Barcelona has only 806 large firms, 433 of which are concentrated in the city of Barcelona (the data are inflated by a headquarter-effect in the city). There has been a considerable increase in the number of medium-sized and large firms in recent times. Thus, the number of medium-sized firms rose from 2,786 in the year 1996 to 4.517 in 2008. The number of large firms rose from 526 to 806.

### 8.1.6    External and Internal Trade

The export of goods from the province has risen 450 per cent between 1991 and 2007, from €7,100 million to €39,000 million (nominal values). Exports of goods from Barcelona to the rest of the world have increased faster than the growth of total EU exports and faster than total exports from the rest of the world, so Barcelona has increased its contribution to EU15 trade and to world trade. Imports of goods have risen to approximately 300 per cent between 1995 and 2007, rising from €15,400 million

*Table 8.4    International and interregional trade*

(a)  International trade: Barcelona province–rest of the world, 1991–2009 (€m)

| Year | Exports of goods | Imports of goods | Balance (X–M) |
|------|------------------|------------------|---------------|
| 1991 | 7,137 | 15,448 | −8,311 |
| 2001 | 30,478 | 42,885 | −12,407 |
| 2007 | 39,837 | 65,885 | −26,047 |
| 2008 | 39,807 | 62,943 | −23,136 |
| 2009 | 32,262 | 48,520 | −16,257 |

*Source:*   Based on AEAT (Agencia Española de Administración Tributaria: Spanish Agency for Tax Administration).

(b)  Interregional trade: Exports of goods from Catalonia to the rest of Spain and imports of goods to Catalonia from the rest of Spain, 2003–2007 (€m)

| Year | Exports | Imports | Balance (X–M) |
|------|---------|---------|---------------|
| 2003 | 43,560 | 25,725 | 17,835 |
| 2007 | 53,207 | 31,278 | 21,930 |

*Source:*   Elaborated from C-Intereg.

to €62,000 million. Despite the higher relative growth rate of exports, the total value of imports has increased more than the value of exports so the negative trade balance rose from €8,300 million to €23,000 million (170 per cent growth rate) (Table 8.4). However, if the fluxes with the rest of Spain are considered (this is effectively to consider the rest of Spain as a foreign country) the export rate becomes positive. This contrasts with the important interregional negative balance of other provinces such as Madrid.

However, after 2007 a consequence of the crisis is a significant reduction in imports, whereas exports have improved. As a result, the negative trade balance has fallen. In 2010, exports and imports are recovering due to an upturn in external demand.

A characteristic of the province of Barcelona is its external openness. Exports of goods and services account for 30 per cent of GDP if the rest of Spain is not taken into account, and 68 per cent if it is. Openness measured as exports plus imports on GDP is about 70 per cent and if the rest of Spain is included as a foreign country the rate rises to 130 per cent. The share of foreign trade outside Spain on GDP is still rising.

### 8.1.7 Foreign Direct Investment (FDI)

Catalonia has shown itself to be one of the most successful regions in Europe at attracting multinational firms. There are more than 3,000 foreign multinationals in Catalonia (600 are manufacturing firms and more than 2,000 are service firms). More than 90 per cent are located in the province of Barcelona, mainly in the metropolitan region of Barcelona (see Section 8.3), whereas 45 per cent have their headquarters in the city of Barcelona. This constitutes 30 per cent of the foreign multinational firms in Spain.

The most important FDI investments are concentrated in motor vehicles, electrical components, chemicals, and food and beverages. Some of these companies are Volkswagen-Audi, SEAT, Endesa, Nestlé, Sanofi Aventis, Schneider electrics and so on. In the 2000–10 period, the annual average FDI inflow has been around €2,200 million and the outflow €4,300 million with an average negative balance of €2,100 million per year. Approximately 80 per cent of flows have origin or destination in OECD countries where 50 per cent belongs to the EU27. Despite these figures, Catalonia does not play the same role in FDI as in external trade in Spain. In the 2000–08 period, Catalonia accounts for only 14 per cent of the Spanish inflows and 11 per cent of the Spanish outflows. This is due to the fact that Madrid's stock market is much more important than Barcelona's, and absorbs most of the Spanish FDI flows.

### 8.1.8 Knowledge Economy

Since 1990, Barcelona has experienced an intense change towards a knowledge-based economy. Employment growth in knowledge-based industries has been faster than in non-knowledge-based industries. Knowledge-based jobs doubled between 1991 and 2007 (from 400,000 to 800,000 jobs). This rise has been especially marked in knowledge-intensive services, creating 420,000 new jobs in the province at an annual growth rate of 6.5 per cent. Since 2007, knowledge-intensive industries seem more prepared to resist the effects of the crisis.

Other indicators point in the same direction. The share of R&D on GDP of Catalonia and the province of Barcelona has risen from 0.79 per cent in 1995 to 1.6 per cent in 2009. Despite this fact, R&D/GDP is still lower than the EU average (1.85). About 63 per cent of the expenditures in R&D belong to firms, which is more than the Spanish average (56 per cent). Since 2004, there has been a significant rise of government expenditure in R&D, increasing from 9.3 to 13.7 per cent. Other elements of the new model are the size of the university system, with 12 research universities and more than 250,000 students, and an increase in the number of patents, designs and trademarks.

The transition to a knowledge economy varies widely in the several parts of the province. The city of Barcelona led this transformation, which is now being extended to other cities in the core of the metropolitan area. However, other parts of the province, in particular the Metropolitan Arc and the rest of the province (see Section 8.3) have barely begun the change to a knowledge economy.

## 8.2  COMPARISON WITH OTHER LARGE PROVINCES (NUTS-3) IN THE EU

The province of Barcelona is the tenth most populated NUTS-3 in the EU, after the Rhine-Ruhr (13.4 million inhabitants), Paris (11.2), Randstad (7.5), Inner London (7.4), Milan (7.4), Munich (6.1), Berlin (6.0), Frankfurt (5.6) and Madrid (5.6) (OECD, 2006) (Table 8.5). Comparison with the largest EU regions using OECD and EUROSTAT data indicates that even though the GDP per capita of the province of Barcelona (€27,600) is

*Table 8.5    Population, GDP per capita and labour productivity in the largest EU regions, 2007*

| Metropolitan region/country | Population (m) | GDP pc in PPPs (€1000) | Labour productivity (€1000) |
|---|---|---|---|
| Rhine-Ruhr, Germany | 13.4 | 30.7 | 74.8 |
| Paris, France | 11.2 | 47.8 | 113.2 |
| Randstad-Holland, Netherlands | 7.5 | 36.8 | 71.8 |
| London, UK | 7.4 | 51.7 | 114.0 |
| Milan, Italy | 7.4 | 39.8 | 86.0 |
| Munich, Germany | 6.1 | 39.4 | 78.4 |
| Berlin, Germany | 6.0 | 23.8 | 55.7 |
| Frankfurt, Germany | 5.6 | 37.6 | 82.8 |
| Madrid, Spain | 5.6 | 32.3 | 67.2 |
| Barcelona, Spain | 4.9 | 27.6* | 62.3 |
| Turin, Italy | 2.2 | 35.8 | 86.6 |

*Note:*   * Updated from EUROSTAT and IDESCAT (Institut d'Estadística de Catalunya: Statistical Institute of Catalonia).

*Sources:*   OECD (2006); OECD.Stats; EUROSTAT.

above the EU average, it is not as high as in other large metropolises such as London (€51,700) or Paris (€47,800). Six other large regions are located in a range between 30,000 and 40,000 euros per capita.

According to the OECD (OECD, 2006) data, the evolution of productivity is particularly worrying since Barcelona (62,300 euros/employee) and Berlin (55,700 euros/employee) show lower labour productivity than the average in the largest EU regions. London (114,000 euros/employee) and Paris (113,000 euros/employee) lead the ranking and their labour productivity is 83 per cent higher than that in Barcelona. Turin, Milan and Frankfurt are in an intermediate position with labour productivity between 80,000 and 90,000 euros/employee, whereas the Munich, Rhine-Ruhr and Randstad figures (between 70,000 and 80,000 euros/employee) are closer to Barcelona.

The structure of employment is quite similar to other EU large areas. The main differences are the importance of the manufacturing and construction sectors. The specialization in manufacturing is similar to Overbayern (Munich, 22.4 per cent) and Rhine-Ruhr (23.8 per cent) and lower than Piedmont (28.3 per cent) and Lombardy (29.3 per cent) (Table 8.6).

Firm size (4.9 employees/unit) is lower than the EU average (six employees). The average firm size is significantly higher in German regions such as Hessen/Frankfurt (24.5 employees/unit), Nordrhein-Westfalen/Rhine-Rhur (24), Oberbayern/Munich (18.2), and Berlin (17.5), as well as other regions such as Inner London (9.5), Noord-Holland/Randstad (8) and Île de France/Paris (6). Only Lombardy (4.1), Piedmont (3.8) and Languedoc-Roussillon (3.5) show a smaller firm size (Table 8.7).

According to EUROSTAT data, the average percent of employees in knowledge-intensive industries (manufacturing and services) in the EU regions is about 40 per cent. All the large regions exceed this average, particularly those in Germany and Île de France, which have more than 50 per cent of their employment in knowledge-intensive sectors. The other large regions, including Barcelona, and also Piedmont and Languedoc-Roussillon have between 40 and 50 per cent of their employment in knowledge-intensive industries (Table 8.8).

The effort in R&D expenditures follows a similar pattern, where most of the largest EU regions exceed the EU average, especially those in Germany (Oberbayern 4.32 per cent, Berlin 3.36 per cent, Hessen 2.63 per cent), as well as Paris-Île de France (3.11 per cent). Languedoc-Roussillon (2.08 per cent) and Madrid (1.92 per cent) are close to the EU average, whereas Piedmont (1.71 per cent), Barcelona (1.47 per cent) and Lombardy (1.11 per cent) are below the EU average (Table 8.9).

*Table 8.6    Employment by sector: largest EU areas, 2007*

| Region | Agriculture, hunting, forestry and fishing | Industry and energy | Con-struction | Services |
|---|---|---|---|---|
| European Union (27 countries) | 5.82 | 19.56 | 7.89 | 66.25 |
| European Union (25 countries) | 4.65 | 19.20 | 7.99 | 67.65 |
| European Union (15 countries) | 3.60 | 18.21 | 8.04 | 69.56 |
| Oberbayern (Munich) | 2.40 | 22.46 | 5.39 | 69.76 |
| Berlin | 0.57 | 10.73 | 5.52 | 83.18 |
| Hessen (Frankfurt) | 1.30 | 21.13 | 5.17 | 72.40 |
| Nordrhein-Westfalen (Rhine-Rhur) | 1.54 | 23.86 | 5.48 | 69.11 |
| Catalonia (Barcelona) | 2.55 | 23.07 | 12.01 | 62.37 |
| Île de France (Paris) | 0.44 | 12.18 | 5.00 | 82.19 |
| Languedoc-Roussillon (L'Hérault) | 5.42 | 9.03 | 8.15 | 77.27 |
| Piedmont (Turin) | 3.69 | 28.36 | 7.51 | 60.44 |
| Lombardy (Milan) | 1.64 | 29.32 | 7.73 | 61.31 |
| Noord-Holland (Randstad) | 2.15 | 9.90 | 5.14 | 78.12 |
| London (inner and outer) | 0.28 | 7.06 | 6.42 | 85.67 |

*Source:*    Elaborations on EUROSTAT.

## 8.3    TERRITORIAL STRUCTURE OF THE PROVINCE OF BARCELONA

### 8.3.1    Territorial Administrative Organization

The province of Barcelona is divided into three basic territorial adminis-trative levels: *vegueries* (Barcelona Metropolitan Ambit; central counties), counties (Alt Penedès, Baix Llobregat, Barcelonès, Garraf, Maresme, Vallès Oriental, Vallès Occidental, Anoia, Bages, Berguedà, Osona) and municipalities (311 municipalities).

However, the real socioeconomic structure of the province is quite dif-ferent. In order to understand this structure we need to see the province of

*Table 8.7    Firm size: largest EU areas, 2007*

| Region | Employees/unit |
|---|---|
| European Union (27 countries) | 6.0 |
| Oberbayern (Munich) | 18.2 |
| Berlin | 17.5 |
| Hessen (Frankfurt) | 24.5 |
| Nordrhein-Westfalen (Rhine-Rhur) | 24.0 |
| Catalonia (Barcelona) | 4.9 |
| Île de France (Paris) | 6.0 |
| Languedoc-Roussillon (L'Hérault) | 3.5 |
| Lombardy (Milan) | 4.1 |
| Piedmont (Turin) | 3.8 |
| Noord-Holland (Randstad) | 8.0 |
| Inner London | 9.5 |

*Source:*   EUROSTAT Structural Business Statistics.

*Table 8.8    Employment in knowledge-intensive industries (manufacturing and services): largest EU areas, 2007*

| Region | Employees in knowledge-intensive industries | % of total employees |
|---|---|---|
| Oberbayern (Munich) | 1,089,830 | 54 |
| Berlin | 796,640 | 53 |
| Hessen (Frankfurt) | 1,461,770 | 52 |
| Nordrhein-Westfalen (Rhine-Rhur) | 3,592,020 | 45 |
| Catalonia | 1,268,460 | 36 |
| Province of Barcelona | 989,719 | 40 |
| Île de France (Paris) | 2,688,540 | 51 |
| Languedoc-Roussillon (L'Hérault) | 375,680 | 40 |
| Lombardy (Milan) | 1,860,750 | 43 |
| Piedmont (Turin) | 783,900 | 42 |
| Noord-Holland (Randstad) | 691,350 | 50 |
| London (inner and outer) | 1,975,250 | 55 |

*Sources:*   Elaborations on EUROSTAT and Ministerio de Trabajo, INSS.

*Table 8.9   R&D expenditures on GDP: largest EU areas, 2007*

| Region | % GDP |
|---|---|
| European Union (27 countries) | 1.85 |
| European Union (15 countries) | 1.93 |
| Oberbayern (Munich) | 4.32 |
| Berlin | 3.36 |
| Hessen (Frankfurt) | 2.63 |
| Nordrhein-Westfalen (Rhine-Rhur) | 1.80 |
| Catalonia (Barcelona) | 1.47 |
| Madrid | 1.92 |
| Île de France (Paris)* | 3.11 |
| Languedoc-Roussillon* (L'Hérault) | 2.08 |
| Lombardy (Milan)** | 1.11 |
| Piedmont (Turin)** | 1.71 |
| Noord-Holland (Randstad) | 1.15 |
| London (inner and outer) | 1.05 |

*Note:*   * Last year available 2004; ** Last year available 2005.

*Source*:   Elaborations on EUROSTAT.

Barcelona from two different points of view. On the one hand the metropolitan areas and local labour markets provide a good picture of the socio-economic area divisions of the province, whereas on the other the design of the networks of cities presents the structure of relations among the municipalities, which are the basic nodes in the province (Roca et al., 2005).

### 8.3.2   The Metropolitan Region of Barcelona

The most outstanding difference is between the metropolitan region of Barcelona and the rest of the province. In 1986 the metropolitan region began a process of economic and territorial expansion that led to it becoming one of the 10 largest urban agglomerations in Europe, with a size similar to the 10th largest North American agglomeration (Washington) and ranked as one of the 30 largest metropolises in the OECD (OECD, 2006, 2009a). It is the second largest metropolitan area in Spain, after Madrid.[1] The territorial expansion has arisen not from a process of hierarchical decentralization but rather as the effect of the increasing interaction

---

[1]   On metropolitan area researches in Spain, see Clusa and Roca, 1997; Salvador et al., 1997; Boix, 2006; Boix and Trullén, 2007; Boix and Veneri, 2009.

between the urban continuum of Barcelona and a group of medium-sized cities that were old industrial centres.

The expansion took place in several ways. Regarding its spatial dimension, the metropolitan region increased from 90 municipalities in 1986 to about 220 in 2006 and increased its spatial area threefold (Map 8.1). Spatial expansion stopped in 1996 for the most part because the boundaries of the metropolitan region of Barcelona reached the boundaries of other metropolitan areas (also in expansion) although population, employment and production still rose due to endogenous growth. The metropolitan region of Barcelona rose from 3.56 million inhabitants in 1986 to 5.2 in 2010, and from 1.04 million jobs in 1986 to 2.2 in 2010 (Boix and Galletto, 2004; Boix and Veneri, 2009). About 100 municipalities do not belong to the real metropolitan region of Barcelona, where 19 form a second small metropolitan area around the city of Manresa, in the inner part of the province.

Although the boundaries of the metropolitan region expanded up to 2001, the most common definition of metropolitan region for planning is the one proposed by the *Pla Territorial Metropolità*, which defines a metropolitan region quite similar to the metropolitan region as it was in 1991, when it covered 164 municipalities (the metropolitan region today covers more than 200). This metropolitan region for planning is usually divided in two parts: first, the core or inner part of the metropolitan region, formerly named 'Barcelona's Metropolitan Strategic Plan' and currently 'Metropolitan Area', comprising Barcelona and 35 other surrounding municipalities; second, the so-called 'Metropolitan Arc' or outer part (the other 128 municipalities) (Map 8.2). Even if smaller in economic terms than the metropolitan area, the economic size of the Metropolitan Arc is similar to the third Spanish metropolitan area (Valencia) and has some important medium-sized cities (Mataró, Granollers, Sabadell, Terrassa and Vilanova i la Geltrú).

### 8.3.3   Local Labour Markets

The identification of local labour market areas (LLMAs) was carried out by Boix and Galletto (2006) for Spain at the request of the Ministry of Industry. This division is not administrative or 'official' but provides valuable information about the internal organization of the socioeconomic dynamics. There are 19 LLMAs centred in the province of Barcelona: Artés, Barcelona, Berga, Calaf, Calella, Capellades, La Garriga, Granollers, Igualada, Manresa, Mataró, Monistrol de Montserrat, Prats de Lluçanès, Sabadell, Sallent, Sant Celoni, Sant Sadurní d'Anoia, Vic and Vilafranca del Penedès (Map 8.2). The largest labour markets are located in the metropolitan region of Barcelona.

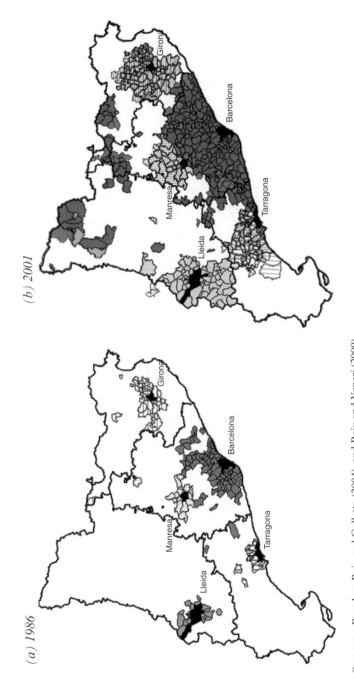

*(a) 1986*

*(b) 2001*

*Sources:* Based on Boix and Galletto (2004), and Boix and Veneri (2009).

*Map 8.1   The process of territorial expansion of metropolitan areas in Catalonia, 1986–2001*

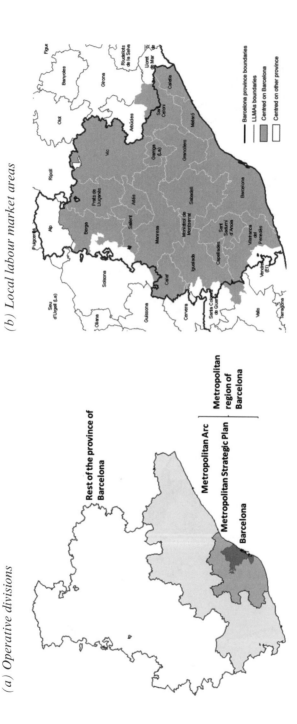

*(a) Operative divisions*

*(b) Local labour market areas*

Barcelona province boundaries
LLMAs boundaries
Centred on Barcelona
Centred on other province

Rest of the province of Barcelona

Metropolitan Arc

Metropolitan Strategic Plan

Metropolitan region of Barcelona

Barcelona

*Sources:* Elaborated from Boix and Galletto (2006) and Trullén and Boix (2006).

*Map 8.2 Operative divisions of the province of Barcelona and local labour market areas*

**8.3.4 Largest Cities**

The most important city is Barcelona (1,621,000 inhabitants) and four other cities have more than 200,000 inhabitants: L'Hospitalet de Llobregat (257,000) and Badalona (220,000) are contiguous to Barcelona, whereas Terrassa (211,000) and Sabadell (206,000) are 25 kilometres from Barcelona and located in the Metropolitan Arc.

Other important cities in the neighbourhood of Barcelona (metropolitan area) are Santa Coloma de Gramanet (122,000 inhabitants), Cornellà de Llobregat (86,000), Sant Boi de Llobregat (82,000) and El Prat de Llobregat (63,000). Other medium-sized cities in the Metropolitan Arc are Mataró (122,000 inhabitants), Sant Cugat del Vallès 79,000), Rubí (73,000), Vilanova i la Geltrú (66,000), Viladecans (63,000), Castelldefels (62.000), Granollers (60,000), Cerdanyola del Vallès (59,000) and Mollet del Vallès (52,000).

The other three small cities in the province of Barcelona with capacity to structure territory from outside the metropolitan region of Barcelona are Igualada (38,000 inhabitants), Manresa (75,000 inhabitants) and Vic (39,000 inhabitants).

The city of Barcelona is the main economic engine of the province. It led the industrial revolution in Spain in 1835, and until 1900 the province accounted for most of the manufacturing production of the Spanish economy. As a consequence of Spanish protectionism, Barcelona's economy experienced a technological and organizational slowdown in comparison with the western European economies, especially during the isolation period of the first stage of the dictatorial regime (1939–59). Since its openness to the international economy starting in 1959, Barcelona has developed a new productive manufacturing base, with a central role for small and medium-sized enterprises, and with a substantial number of industrial multinational companies. The capacity for attracting population and economic activity led to intense metropolitan growth. The crisis of the 1970s and the political transition meant the end of a development model based on low capital-intensive production, very intensive in low-qualified labour and basically oriented to protect the domestic market. The city of Barcelona has experienced an intensive process of economic transformation since 1986, due to the effects of Spain's entry into the European Economic Community and its nomination to host the Olympic Games.

The city of Barcelona also leads the processes of growth and internationalization of the province. Since 1997, the change in its economic base has been built of the notion of 'Barcelona as a knowledge city' (Trullén, 2000). About 50 per cent of the productive structure is devoted to

*(a) Four director flows, 2001*                    *(b) Four director flows without Barcelona, 2001*

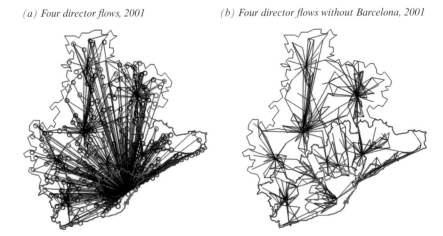

*Sources:*   Elaborated from Trullén and Boix (2000, 2008).

*Map 8.3    Networks of cities in the province of Barcelona*

knowledge-intensive activities. The new strategy of the city is represented by the so-called '22@bcn project', a project to transform approximately 140 hectares (with a buildable area of 4 million square metres) in the centre of the city (in the Poblenou district) and change the old manufacturing uses of this sector of the city to knowledge-intensive activities. The transformation of the city also involves new infrastructure and urban projects such as the continuation of the Diagonal Avenue up to the sea, enlarging the airport and the port, the rerouting (of the course) of the Llobregat River, the high-speed train, and several new underground lines. This strategy is currently being extended to the rest of the metropolitan area.

### 8.3.5   Polycentric Networks of Cities

Such a dense and populated metropolitan region and the great number of large, medium-sized and small cities structuring the territory configures a polycentric network of cities well-weaved around some of the old industrial subcentres and other newer industrial cities (Map 8.3). This space cannot be simply understood as a 'belt' as the subcentres are not satellites of Barcelona and the network is highly complex. Despite this fact, several parts of the Metropolitan Arc appear to be poorly connected. This design shows not only the location of the subcentres that configure the metropolitan territory but also the deficiencies in the infrastructure in several parts of the technological arc that are currently being improved. The city of Barcelona serves as a common nexus connecting these spaces because the system of infrastructures continues to be highly radial. Furthermore, there is not a true difference between the centre of the metropolitan region (metropolitan area) and the Metropolitan Arc.

### 8.3.6 Urban/Rural Characteristics

The province of Barcelona is classified by the OECD (OECD, 2009a) as predominantly urban since the average population density is 700 hab/km$^2$ and 99.4 per cent of the population live at least 45 minutes by road from cities in the province of Barcelona of more than 50,000 inhabitants such as Manresa and Terrassa. However, not all the municipalities of the province are considered to be urban. In fact, there is a clear distinction between the metropolitan region of Barcelona and the rest of the province. The metropolitan region comprises the municipalities with the highest density in the province, and only some specific parts of the counties of Penedès and the Vallès Oriental could be classified as rural. In the other part of the province, density is lower so that, with the exception of the medium-sized cities (Igualada, Manresa, Vic, Berga) and some surrounding municipalities, the majority of the other part of the province exhibits rural characteristics in terms of density. This explains in part why the networks of cities are very hierarchical in this non-metropolitan part of the province (Map 8.3).

Regarding the local labour markets, most of them are classified as urban according to OECD criteria because the 'urbanity' of medium-sized cities and the weight of the population in their labour markets counterbalances the 'rurality' of the small municipalities (OECD, 2009a). Only three small local labour markets (Sallent, Prats de Lluçanès and Monistrol de Montserrat) could be classified as rural. The total population of these small labour markets is less than 30,000 inhabitants.

## 8.4 CONCLUSIONS

In this chapter we have presented the most important features of the province of Barcelona: the fast employment growth between 1986 and 2007 (but with slow productivity growth), the small average size of local firms, the external openness, the transformation towards the knowledge-based economy, and the intense process of convergence in GDP per capita that has taken place in the last 15 years.

The core of the province is the metropolitan region of Barcelona, which has gone through a process of economic and territorial expansion, started in the mid-1980s. The important fact is that this expansion has arisen not from a process of hierarchical decentralization but rather as the effect of the increasing interaction between the urban continuum of Barcelona and a group of medium-sized cities that were old industrial centres. Nowadays, the metropolitan region and the great number of large, medium-sized and small cities structuring the territory configures a polycentric network of cities well-weaved around some of the old industrial subcentres and other newer industrial cities.

These characteristics of the province of Barcelona have allowed it to benefit from the external economies of localization, the urbanization economies generated by the scale of the metropolitan diversity, and finally to network economies derived from the existence of a network of cities generating synergies. The extension and deepening of the territorial inter-action will be the base of the scenarios of future development depicted in Chapter 10.

# PART IV

# Policy recommendations for regional development

# 9.  Policy options for the Latin Arc

## Roberto Camagni

## 9.1   GENERAL CONSIDERATIONS AND NATIONAL POLICY TASKS

The present post-crisis context of advanced economies is profoundly characterized by a re-launching of public intervention in the economic field, in the form of:

- rescue policies, especially in the financial field as the crisis broke,
- short-term, anti-cyclical policies intended to boost internal demand and mainly involving the building, construction and infrastructure sectors (still in an early post-crisis phase),
- drafting new rules and regulations mainly concerning control over financial risks and most speculative financial products, and
- long-term, structural policies intended to strengthen production sectors and their orientation towards new technologies and new production paradigms.

One of the most important efforts in economic policy making for the years to come will concern – according to the EU as well – strengthening the link between short- and long-term interventions, to be achieved through what are increasingly called 'smart investments'. The general aim should be to revitalize internal demand while at the same time boosting the local and national competitiveness of the production system.

Of course, in the recent evolution of the post-crisis period, a new and stringent constraint has emerged, and it is linked to the critical condition of public deficits and debts. In a sense, the crisis, which started mainly in the financial context and then hit the 'real' economic one, is bringing financial issues back to the forefront, with the difficulties, costs and risks taken by sovereign debts on the financial markets. This obviously implies a much more stringent path out of the crisis, with the impossibility of enlarging public expenditure and the need to commit a rising share of private savings to the re-launching of investments and to backing public policies.

On a scenario time span extending until 2025, the necessary structural policies become central, and in fact they represent a constituent and consistent part of the scenarios presented and elaborated in the present study. Even in the reference scenario, they are present in the form of support to the emergence of a new production paradigm – that of the green economy – orienting in a consistent and synergic direction both public and private investments. But, of course, the centrality of long-sighted, visionary and intentional policies is most visible in the proactive scenario, where a full perception and even anticipation of structural change underway is hypothesized by policy makers, and a close involvement in new policy goals and styles is considered.

However, linking short- and long-term goals and tools is not the only requirement for effective economic and structural policies. A similar consistency is required among the actions of different government levels, from the Community to the national, regional and local ones. This goal can be achieved through explicit coordination efforts ('multilevel governance') or through implicit synergetic behaviour whereby each policy layer operates with its own instruments and inside its own competences adopting a fully complementary attitude. This requisite cooperative behaviour implies, in operational terms, two main elements:

- high permeability between policy layers, in particular linking top-down processes of policy design, programming and financial support with bottom-up processes of project design and operational implementation; and
- the importance of local policies acting on the different aspects of territorial capital and implemented through inclusionary processes of vision building and project elaboration.

The main areas of policy design and implementation relate to two broad fields: (aggregate but also local) demand policies, and (regionalized) supply policies.

### 9.1.1 Demand Policies

1. The most urgent part of demand policies concerns the design of an exit strategy from the present deficit of member states' budgets, reducing reliance on public expenditure. Direct public intervention through public consumption and investment should be substituted by less expensive, indirect public expenditure – for example, in the form of incentives to private demand – or by appropriate regulatory policies. In this case, rather than simply trying to force an anticipation

of private expenditure on durable goods, such as cars and electrical appliances, the goal of supporting private demand could be achieved, in the fields of building and construction, through incentives for energy-saving solutions and cautious deregulation policies. In the case of those sectors in which monopoly positions still persist, for instance telecommunications and many private, trade and professional services, the same goal could be achieved through support for new demand fields, such as cultural and education services.

2.  The creation of new sources of aggregate demand, such as the opening up of new international markets in developing countries. This strategy entails trade agreements with these countries concerning both their internal markets and the EU market, for example, in the agricultural products field; support for their development policies through multiple forms of cooperation; and in the case of emerging countries with huge surpluses in their trade balances, joint international efforts to reach agreement on a cautious but steady re-evaluation of their currencies.

3.  Full support for the launching of new production paradigms implying multiple technological advances, multiple applications in a wide array of sectors, and multiple possibilities of product innovations. The case of the green economy paradigm is the perfect example: its emergence could be supported by appropriate environmental regulations and some public financial support. It encompasses a wide spectrum of innovations, affecting sectors such as energy production, building and construction, advanced R&D and manufacturing activities, transport and agriculture. In the last case, an interesting example concerns the recent spread of the 'zero-km-agriculture' model, which implies only a change in public perceptions and preferences, and enables the achievement of important reductions in transport emissions and costs, new agricultural organization and local markets, and easier defence of peri-urban agricultural land against urbanization and real estate speculation.

4.  The conquest of new internal and international markets through the enhanced competitiveness of local production. Appropriate strategies at the macroeconomic level concern cautious wage increases, (facilitated) private investments in technology, organization and management culture, and a focus on advanced and excellence production. This strategy, however, can be widely supported by supply actions implemented mainly at the regional and local levels.

5.  Intelligent use of the existing public procurement of goods and services, although this is due to shrink, for the creation of an initial market for advanced, environment-friendly products in the building and

construction sector, in advanced telecommunications networks and services, and in the provision of many e-services such as health, social assistance, and e-governance in general.

### 9.1.2 Supply Policies

Supply policies mainly concern the efficiency and innovativeness of the production system, which, in its turn, depends largely on national context elements but also, and particularly, on local context elements.

National policy actions concern the general cultural and educational contexts of countries, the main internal infrastructure networks, the general regulatory framework in the field of anti-trust and land-use controls, the structure of industrial incentives and regional policies. All these elements are particularly important in the achievement of the general goal, already mentioned, of driving rapid recovery from the crisis by reorienting production towards more advanced and more innovative sectors, products and firms. Selective fiscal policies allowing the de-taxing of firms' investments, but also far-looking regulatory policies with regard to the environmental characteristics of production processes, products and living standards (heating, mobility, energy production), may greatly facilitate the necessary intersectoral reallocation of resources.

The second task assigned to these national, supply-side policies concerns wide investments with an interregional scope. Cooperation among regional governments (or among states in federal systems) seems particularly difficult to achieve in the provision of large infrastructure networks, in the management of large river and hydro-geological basins, and in the design of integrated, network strategies for tourism.

In this field, the role of national governments is still crucial, coupled with an important lobbying role of leading regional governments. An important case was found during this research work: the transport integration of the Latin Arc regions. In fact, the western Mediterranean macro-region, in spite of the many common characteristics and the sharing of the sea resource, still exhibits striking fragmentation in terms of mobility infrastructure (and consequently, in terms of economic integration). This fragmentation is even more striking if compared with the clear interregional and also international integration strategy pursued and implemented in the northern part of the EU, in the area of the large, leading capital city-regions (London–Paris–Brussels–Randstad Holland–Berlin–Frankfurt), and with the historical territorial integration of the large central European axis running along the Rhine, the so-called 'blue banana'. In particular, along the southern belt the condition of the rail infrastructure is not at all satisfactory. Long-standing technical problems between the French and Spanish rail systems, difficulties in the Liguria and southern Italian regions, lack of priority in the French southern east–west axis, and the clear priorities given in almost all countries to north–south connections linking the large Mediterranean ports with their continental hinterlands: all these have prevented the implementation of an efficient Mediterranean network, reinforcing the historical lack of cooperation among the European southern regions.

Similarities among these Mediterranean regions were long deemed more important than potential complementarities, and this led to explicit competition in tourism, maritime transport and agriculture. Today, however, an increasing differentiation is emerging – among regions and among cities – which may give rise to greater interregional specialization and the consequent integration of the respective markets. In policy terms, the possibility is also present for exploring closer interregional cooperation in the form of 'synergy networks' (Camagni, 1993; Camagni and Salone, 1993; Camagni and Capello, 2004): among ports, with a commodity and branch specialization; in the spheres of tourism, building – and selling in the global market – integrated 'itineraries' in both maritime cruise and city/ cultural tourism; and among knowledge centres for cooperation on R&D and advanced education.

But another relevant potential for supply-side policies exists, and implies important responsibilities for regional and local governments. Here the focus of action is on the accumulation and best utilization of 'territorial capital', which, as indicated by an important statement by DG Regio of the EU Commission, is still not sufficiently elaborated by either the scientific or the operative policy milieus:

> Each Region has a specific 'territorial capital' that is distinct from that of other areas and generates a higher return for specific kinds of investments than for others, since these are better suited to the area and use its assets and potential more effectively. Territorial development policies (policies with a territorial approach to development) should first and foremost help areas to develop their territorial capital. (CEC, 2005, p. 1)

## 9.2 THE CONCEPT OF TERRITORIAL CAPITAL AND ITS RELEVANCE FOR REGIONAL POLICY STRATEGIES

The concept of territorial capital was first proposed in a regional policy context by the OECD in its *Territorial Outlook* (OECD, 2001). This set out a well-structured list of factors acting as determinants of territorial capital and ranging from traditional material assets to more recent non-material ones:

These factors may include the area's geographical location, size, factor of production endowment, climate, traditions, natural resources, quality of life or the agglomeration economies provided by its cities, but may also include its business incubators and industrial districts or other business networks that reduce transaction costs. Other factors may be 'untraded interdependencies' such as understandings, customs and informal rules that enable economic actors to work together under conditions of uncertainty, or the solidarity, mutual assistance and co-opting of ideas that often develop in clusters of small and medium-sized enterprises working in the same sector (social capital). Lastly, according to Marshall, there is an intangible factor, 'something in the air', called the 'environment' and which is the outcome of a combination of institutions, rules, practices, producers, researchers and policy makers that make a certain creativity and innovation possible. (OECD, 2001, p. 15)

Although it is clear that some items in the above list belong to the same abstract factor class and differ only in terms of the theoretical approaches of their proponents, and some others are lacking, the concept appears to be sound and fruitful. A full and possibly complete taxonomy of elements of territorial capital has been presented elsewhere (Camagni, 2009), underlining the three main dichotomies encompassed by the concept:

- material and non-material elements: social overhead capital, infrastructure, public goods and private fixed capital on the one hand, and human capital, entrepreneurship and social capital on the other. Agglomeration and urbanization economies exhibit a mix of both elements;
- private and public goods, but also an intermediate category of impure public goods and club goods, for which new governance styles are required. In fact, in order to prevent opportunistic behaviour by some actors and excessive exploitation of 'commons' and public goods, there is a need for new policy styles addressed to the creation of wide public consensus, reciprocal trust, synergies and cooperation; and
- functional and relational elements, the latter constituting the most novel and most interesting development factors today. Relational assets, in the form of interpersonal and inter-institutional linkages, represent a 'capital' because they are costly to construct and maintain, but they facilitate innovation, creativity and the enhancement of economic competitiveness.

Acting on territorial capital in policy making means acknowledging the integrated nature of any policy strategy, the added value of intervening in different but linked assets at the same time, promoting network relations and cooperative agreements, and supporting innovative projects emerging through partnerships among industry, research institutions and universities instead of supporting the single partners directly.

For the sake of simplicity, we may envisage four large classes of territorial capital elements to which attention should be given in a policy context:

- *infrastructure capital and settlement structure*, encompassing also the characteristics of the urban system and the quality of the environment;
- *cognitive capital*, in the form of knowledge, skills, capabilities, educational and research structure, embedded in both productive and human capital;
- *cultural and identitarian capital*, encompassing cultural heritage, landscape and natural capital; and
- *social and relational capital*, in the form of civicness, associative willingness and cooperation capability.

## 9.3 LOCAL AND REGIONAL POLICIES: ACTING THROUGH 'TERRITORIAL PLATFORMS'

As mentioned, regional supply-side policy strategies should explicitly address the conservation, best use, completion and improvement of the various forms of territorial capital. The main messages in this case are the necessity to integrate traditional spatial development policies into each territory more closely through the harmonious merging of material and non-material elements, functional and relational assets, economic, social and environmental aspects; to create new cooperation networks among local actors, and among them, policy makers and external bodies, endeavouring to create willing and cohesive local communities; and to focus on excellence assets in the spheres of knowledge, culture, natural and cultural heritage, and support innovation through synergetic behaviour (Camagni, 2009; Camagni and Maillat, 2006).

This integration strategy can be synthesized into the concept of 'territorial platforms', a concept recently used by the Italian government to depict its 'territorialization' strategy (wise integration into territorial specificities) concerning infrastructure and development actions. Intervening through territorial platforms means seeking to achieve a close match and full integration – in functional, physical, economic, social and aesthetic terms – between new development projects and the local realm, at the same time mobilizing multiple local resources in support and synergy with public action.

In parallel with the broad categories of territorial capital already mentioned, we may envisage three main platforms – *infrastructure platforms*, *knowledge platforms* and *identity platforms* – while the fourth category of territorial capital, namely 'relational' capital, may be considered as the provider of a fourth platform, a *governance platform*, at the same time a sort of precondition for success of public action and a new policy implementation style. The different possible actions pertaining to the three forms of platforms are illustrated in Map 9.1.

### 9.3.1   Infrastructure Platforms

New infrastructure platforms will enable the achievement of some basic priorities for the Latin Arc, namely: improving the internal integration of the entire area; boosting the external accessibility of each region with respect to the Latin Arc and external territories, in order to achieve enhanced competitiveness and attractiveness; and improving the internal efficiency of large metropolitan areas through a polynuclear urban structure.

New infrastructure platforms encompass (Map 9.1):

- a better and integrated rail network along the entire Latin Arc, as already stated;
- the use of new 'highways of the sea' in order to achieve the same goal;
- improved linkages of larger metropolitan areas with the main European corridors: the Corridor of the Two Seas (Genoa–Rotterdam); links with Corridor 1 (through the proposed new rail and road axis TI-Bre, Tirreno-Brenner from La Spezia to Parma, Verona and the Brenner); Corridor 8 (Naples–Bari–Patras); improved infrastructure linking Barcelona with Marseilles, Lyon, Turin and the Po Valley, Strasbourg and Central Europe; and
- an orbital railway system internal to the Barcelona metropolitan area, allowing the structuring of a strong ring of subcentres (see following subsections).

### 9.3.2   Knowledge Platforms

Knowledge platforms consist of cooperation networks among the main actors in the knowledge society: advanced research institutions, higher education institutions, advanced and dynamic firms. Local firms are not only the recipients of the output of the specialized knowledge plexus (institutions working on scientific and applied research); they also possess long-standing local production competence and know how:

*Map 9.1   Policy actions and 'territorial platforms'*

Legend:
- Competence poles
- Knowledge platforms
- Identity platforms
- Infrastructure platforms
- Highways of the sea
- Barcelona orbital rail
- Infrastructure integration of the Latin Arc

they are consequently crucial partners in any innovation and technological advancement strategy. Particular attention should be paid by policy makers not only to achieving fruitful cooperation among these three local actors (in line with the hitherto successful experience of the French '*poles de compétitivité*'), but also to monitoring the persistence of local production knowledge, which might be jeopardized by the selective delocalization of parts of production *filières*.

Knowledge platforms may be structured through (Map 9.1):

- synergy and cooperation among the above-mentioned main actors of the knowledge society into what may be called local 'competence poles'. Examples of such poles now existing or developing are provided by Seville (bio-technologies and links with the agri-food *filière*), Valencia (mechanical engineering for light sectors), Barcelona (wide array of sectors), Montpellier (bio-technologies and green technologies), Nice (information and communication technologies: ICTs), Genoa (ICTs and medical appliances), Turin (industrial automation), Pisa (advanced physical applications), Florence and Bologna (mechanical engineering, bio-medical appliances), and Catania (ICTs);
- the enlargement of cooperation in the applied scientific field between local competence poles and similar but complementary realities in the wider urban region, or even outside it. This strategy could be realized by engaging the entire Catalonian territory or the Genoa–Turin–Milan triangle;
- the inclusion of innovative firms in these cooperation agreements, working on the industrial 'vocations' and the specificities of territories. Examples range from marine technologies, which are highly advanced and incorporated by the local shipbuilding industry in the Genoa–La Spezia–Viareggio–Livorno arc, to mechanical engineering and industrial automation competences on the Bologna–Florence axis; and
- the development of other *filières* linking local natural and productive assets of excellence with knowledge and competence poles. The agri-food-tourism *filière* has huge potential benefits in the Latin Arc area. Similar virtuous circles, building on local 'vocations' and supplying wide potential synergies, concern the health and wellness *filière*, where they link local expertise in medical technologies with the increasing specialization in wellness services and accommodation facilities for a growing population of European retirees. A last example concerns possible increasing engagement with the green economy paradigm, particularly in the supply of bio-mass and

solar energy linked with the production and servicing of new energy technologies.

### 9.3.3 Identity Platforms

Identity platforms exploit natural wealth and local cultural heritage for the development of new economic and employment opportunities. Local identities may become effective 'brands' for new, selective and sustainable forms of tourism, but also for the advertising of ancient local skills embedded in food and wine production and in local handicraft products. An integrated strategy linking all the preceding elements with new physical accessibilities, careful site information, worldwide marketing and enhanced logistic receptivity may prove extremely effective.

Local identities should be rediscovered and interpreted on a wide area level; individual items of cultural heritage should be linked together in larger 'itineraries' integrated in both informational and logistic terms, in order to reach appropriate critical mass and new visibility on the international tourist market.

In the definition of identity platforms, the role of citizens and local population is crucial, because they furnish their sense of belonging and pride of place, their values and expectations, adding real culture and life to what could easily become a trivial commodification of the local atmosphere. Moreover, they are the natural beneficiaries not just of the new employment potential, but also of the improvements that a wise development strategy could bring in terms of accessibility and services.

As shown by Map 9.1, the possibilities of devising identity platforms along the Latin Arc are ample and extremely rich: diversities are widespread, but also the commonalities brought by history and geography are clear.

# 10. Policy scenarios for the province of Barcelona

## Joan Trullén

## 10.1 INTRODUCTION

In this chapter a policy prospect for the Barcelona area is provided, both with reference to economic and spatial strategies, taking into consideration the three integrated scenarios presented in Chapter 3.[1]

With 2025 as our time horizon, these scenarios must be considered in terms of economic and territorial dynamics for the Barcelona metropolis. The main aim consists in making Barcelona a global metropolis by enlarging the radius of its labour market. This will mean the incorporation of cities that are beyond the province of Barcelona such as Girona and Reus-Tarragona-Valls.

From an economic point of view, the fundamental change is to substitute a model based on low productivity and high levels of employment for one of enhanced productivity and apply this alternative model of growth to the urban agglomeration of Barcelona.

It must be emphasized that the implementation of active policies of local development are needed for each scenario. In the case of the reference scenario, active policies will be less intense and targeted than in the proactive scenario, but more focused and better targeted than in the defensive scenario. In all scenarios, the monitoring of active local-level policies is a necessary condition in order to achieve high levels of productivity and employment growth.

---

[1] This section benefits from contributions and suggestions that emerged during workshops and conferences with experts and policy makers organized in the last phases of the research.

## 10.2   SCENARIOS AND POLICIES FOR THE PROVINCE OF BARCELONA

### 10.2.1   Scenarios

We have identified four major strategic economic and territorial factors in four sub-areas of the province of Barcelona:

- those that affect the nature of production, its sectoral composition, its composition in terms of knowledge intensity and technological level and territorial origin of demand;
- those that affect the dynamics of local labour markets, especially those related to the interaction with the central metropolitan labour market;
- those that affect the provision of infrastructure, especially those related to transport and communications infrastructure; and
- those that affect supply factors, in the labour market (education) and technology (R&D).

The main issues concerning the future of the Barcelona area may be explained as follows:

1.  As far as the economic future is concerned, the most relevant question, in the opinion of many experts, is how to transform the economy from low productivity activities to a high value-added economy.
2.  In the territorial field, the province of Barcelona has two great opportunities: (i) to develop the Metropolitan Arc as a place connecting the central area of Barcelona with the cities of central Catalonia, and (ii) to develop a network of municipalities as a tool to reach consensus with agents located in the territory.
3.  Another key question is how to manage the appeal of the province of Barcelona: that Barcelona has special appeal is not in question, but the challenge is to move away from mass tourism to higher-quality tourism.
4.  The fourth priority is to enhance communication networks between Catalan cities. Although it is true that much has been invested in major cities and in the high-speed train, there is very little in communication networks between smaller cities and between industrial areas.
5.  Finally, a major problem is the high level of youth unemployment. During the last 10 years young people have had the opportunity to stop studying and start working immediately in the building sector, with no training. Now they are unemployed, poorly educated and in danger of becoming part of a 'lost generation'. This is a very important problem because it is essential to have human capital to succeed

in the knowledge economy. The role of public administration is key to carrying out this transformation.

### 10.2.2  Policy Proposals

Once the three scenarios have been presented, a new generation of local development policies for municipalities of Barcelona province can be put forward in accordance with the diagnosis made earlier.

The new local development strategy is based upon three basic assumptions. First, the promotion of local development and the reduction of imbalances must take the territorial features into consideration. Second, not only do firms compete but cities do too and therefore the strategy to enhance productivity must have a territorial feature and, more importantly, a local development feature. Third, economic, social and environmental sustainability must have a territorial basis, be this urban or metropolitan. Therefore, this strategy must proceed in two fundamental and integrated ways: by promoting economic development and by enhancing territorial development.

In the reference scenario, development policies that strengthen productivity through improvements in human capital and technological infrastructure will be incorporated. In this scenario the current industrial export-based model is strengthened but there is no structural change in the industrial and productive base.

In the proactive scenario, faster productivity growth is assumed, due to greater investment in human capital, technological capital and infrastructures, but a strong emphasis is given to change at the economic base. The scenario is implemented through a much wider set of economic and territorial policies based on the existence of an important agglomeration in the economy of Barcelona province as a whole.

In the defensive scenario, it is assumed that there are no substantial changes to either the productive basis or the infrastructure. Local development policies do not have a special role. Nor is there a real change in the supply of infrastructures.

### Reference scenario

In this scenario an improvement is assumed in the provision of transport and communications infrastructure that will affect both the connections to all major nodes of the Catalan network of cities and the connections to the rest of the world. It also assumes that the building of the entire road and rail infrastructure will have been concluded (La Sagrera Station; the connection between Barcelona's seaport and the French border with European rail gauge). This increase in the supply of infrastructure is a key requirement in order to increase the efficiency of the whole economy of the province of Barcelona.

The enhancement of total factor productivity, derived from training, R&D and innovation, will be another key area of policy intervention. The basic idea is to coordinate the provision of research and education infrastructure within a network of cities, linking these infrastructures with the technological trajectory of the different cities and with the needs of the environment.

In this scenario, the productive model is strengthened by the existence of a solid export-led industrial base and of provision of services, especially of tourism services. The dynamics of the spatial localization of activities follows a general model of a polycentric metropolis. The metropolis grows in attraction capacity but reduces its physical absorptive capacity, triggering concentric circle urban growth dynamics. From the centre of the metropolis (Barcelona city) the activities expand towards the nearest concentric rings around the cities. Business activities with lower added value and intensive land use tend to relocate towards successive rings under the pressure of higher land prices. Progressively, the Metropolitan Arc receives higher value-added activities, but with a level of employment per unit of surface that it is still low.

Industry relocates towards the next concentric ring of cities and its neighbourhood: Igualada, Manresa and Vic. Some industrial establishments will relocate in these areas from the central metropolis, together with low value-added activities, traditional industrial activities; and also new multinational firms that seek proximity to Barcelona's seaport and the rail connection to the markets of Central Europe. But on the whole there is a growing demand as a result of the expansion of the metropolis and the expansion of the end-markets for industrial products: Barcelona becomes a large central metropolis for a large European region that extends from Alacant to Lyon. Therefore, there will be an increase in productivity but these increases will not be as large as in the proactive scenario.

What needs emphasizing here is that in *this* scenario there is the political will to prevent urban sprawl and to promote and support different cities that constitute the polycentric metropolis. This is consistent with the territorial planning framework (the Metropolitan Territorial Plan of Barcelona) which integrates environmental sustainability goals by developing urban centres.

**Proactive scenario**
In the proactive scenario, specific local and territorial policies will be implemented to ease the transition towards a more knowledge-intensive model with higher productivity levels. These policies must include two

interlinked aspects: economic development (particularly local economic policies) and territorial development (policies which have a local aspect but also have a pronounced regional or metropolitan dimension). One strategy of fundamental importance is the implementation of active industrial policies as well as the support of primary and tertiary activities which focus on new eco-innovative markets.

In particular, the fragmentation of labour markets will be tackled with infrastructure and endogenous development policies so as to foster a new development pattern based on high value-added activities in segments of medium- or high-technological intensity. Therefore we propose the implementation of an integrated economic and territorial strategy to strengthen the network of cities as a whole. In this sense, the integration of the labour markets of the whole province of Barcelona must be accompanied by transport infrastructure policies and in particular railways, which go beyond connecting these cities with the main high-speed rail (Sants–La Sagrera), seaport and airport hubs.

Policies in this scenario must include the construction of the new orbital (rail) line linking Mataró with Vilanova i la Geltrú as a priority linking important centres such as Granollers, Sabadell, Terrassa, Martorell and Vilafranca del Penedès. Similarly, and of great importance is the widening of the transversal (road) axis and the rail link between Girona and Lleida, connecting the Vic–Manresa–Igualada axis.

These two great territorial axes make it possible to enhance the growth of the metropolis from areas beyond its core. Obviously there is a great force located in the nucleus of Barcelona and the metropolitan area (36 contiguous municipalities). But there is the political will to develop new forces that counterbalance this centre: the network of orbital cities and the central area of the transversal axis. Similarly, it is important to note that in this scenario the promotion of the nodes (the orbital cities and the Lleida–Igualada–Manresa–Vic–Girona axis) must take the development of each of these cities in a knowledge-intensive economy as its starting point: they are not simply the receptors of activity from the centre or the result of the expansion of the centre of the metropolis. They are stimulated by specific local economic policies.

*Local policies to promote change in the productive model* The proactive scenario implies in-depth support for local economic policy. The goal is for local economic policy to enable the transition from a low productivity model and closed labour markets (often limited to the municipality borders) to a high productivity model and integrated inter-municipality labour markets. Local economic policy should not aim at the protection or the promotion of small municipal labour markets. On the contrary, the new strategy aims to take full advantage of the existence (and increased strength) of large inter-municipal and regional labour markets. This vision must be extended to the provision of local public services. The scenario assumes ample coordination between municipalities, and increased specialization of each one in the provision of specific services. The provision of public services could enhance the growth of productivity levels.

In this scenario policies of economic development and strategic planning are implemented at inter-municipal or metropolitan level, through a strategy of local cooperation. Employment policies too are defined in a coordinated way and at inter-municipal level, and this runs counter to the traditional local level view.

The local dimension is paramount in the design of a new development model based on agglomeration economies which are linked to large labour markets, large transport and communication infrastructure, a wide range of universities and research centres, and a broad and diversified production system with large industrial plants. The agglomeration of Barcelona amounts to about 5 million inhabitants, and is part of a Catalan economy which has 7.5 million inhabitants and accounts for 20 per cent of the Spanish GDP: this agglomeration is made up of a multiplicity of integrated and interlinked local centres.

This proactive scenario proposes the promotion of agglomeration economies on the basis of three large sets of policies:

1.  policies that promote 'urbanization' economies, with the aim of seeking advantages related to the growth of the urban size and related to the growth of productivity as a result of production diversification;
2.  policies that promote 'localization' economies, targeted at the enhancement of advantages related to the specialization in knowledge-intensive activities; and
3.  policies that promote network economies and territorial interdependence, targeted at strengthening accessibility and ties among cities without the need to enlarge urban size or increase physical proximity.

First, local economic policies targeted at the promotion of urbanization economies underline the fact that productivity growth is related to urban size. An increase in scale allows the emergence of increasing returns, fostering production specialization and promoting diversity.

In the proactive scenario, the policies of delivery of local public services seek scale economies. An important part of local facilities are scaled to inter-municipal dimensions; coordination in the delivery of public services, infrastructure and facilities are specifically and intentionally sought after. The aim is to go beyond the local market in order to lower the costs of the service delivery and to benefit from scale and scope economies. The rationalization of costs becomes fundamental, particularly the fixed costs in the delivery of services.

Employment policies are also implemented largely at an inter-municipal level, making the integration of local labour markets easier, with dual consequences: promoting diversity, specialization and change in higher productivity sectors. In this scenario a municipal strategy for the preservation of local employment, low value-added activities and consequently low salaries is not sought after. The transition towards higher value-added activities is based on a strategy of local labour markets enlargement and integration.

Furthermore, the integration of the transport and communications networks allows smaller municipalities to benefit from the advantages related to the metropolitan level. Special plans to ensure accessibility to major transport and communication infrastructures are designed.

Municipal urbanism also follows criteria that ensure higher interdependence and better connectivity, taking full advantage of the benefits derived from the existence of a metropolitan or regional planning framework. Industrial parks and other urban tools are coordinated by municipalities, in the search for the emergence of externalities related to market dimension and territorial quality.

Therefore, urbanism is at the service of the transformation of the productive base and the exploitation of the advantages derived from the increased scale and productive diversity.

Second, local economic policies that are targeted at the promotion of localization economies. In this proactive scenario, the promotion of localization economies (rooted in production specialization) differs from strategies in use in the twentieth century. The aim is to achieve productivity gains related to externalities provided by the territory. The emphasis is not on specialization in traditional activities, but in new knowledge-intensive activities.

At present, economic policy for endogenous development based on traditional Marshallian 'industrial districts' or on traditional 'clusters' must cede to new development strategies based on knowledge-intense activities (Trullén and Boix, 2000, 2008; Boix and Trullén, 2010). An important example of this kind of strategic change can be found in Barcelona: the strategy to transform the Poblenou district. This former industrial district was transformed into an area based on knowledge economy activities by means of a new programme '22@ Barcelona'. This policy was accompanied by changes in land use established in the *Urban Planning for Barcelona*.

The goal is similar to the traditional one: to develop productivity growth strategies linked to the territory, where small and medium-sized firms abound, so that innovation capabilities are improved.

But the focus now is on new, advanced activities, specifically, the substitution of the old industrial zoning for a new land-use planning based on knowledge will be achieved by means of a special zoning policy that seeks to attract activities to the cities in the Metropolitan Arc and the rest of the province of Barcelona as well. This new urbanism will be implemented with the goal of attracting activities with the following features:

- increased employment density: this means activities that are not land intensive, as they were for the most part in the nineteenth century, but activities which benefit from centrality and at the same time from spatial interaction;
- pronounced use of information and communication technologies;
- highly educated and skilled workforce, based on talent attraction capacity and not on low salaries;
- need for public transport and accessibility to the large metropolitan transport infrastructures (intercontinental airport, seaport, high-speed train stations, freight railway with European gauge to the French border and to the Algeciras/Mediterranean Corridor);
- high urban quality with much lower land costs than those existing in the core of the metropolitan centre;
- emphasis on environmental sustainability; and
- coordination with a new generation of clusters and industrial districts development policies, such as those introduced by the Spanish government in the Innovative Business Groups Programme.

One of the new factors of economic growth is the attraction of company headquarters and innovative establishments, based on technological as well as on non-technological innovation. Global firms are interested in locating these activities in global metropolises but not necessarily in the central core or in the first metropolitan ring but rather in rural places with a high environmental quality and relative proximity to important metropolitan transport infrastructure.

The attraction of technological, educational or legal headquarters of multinational firms contrasts with the present trend to locate low knowledge-intensive activities in rural spaces with a high-quality environment. In this scenario, traditional rural municipalities have to avoid the historical trap of attracting low value-added activities and move in the opposite direction by promoting quality of life and quality of the environment as an enticement for multinationals and large firms.

The transition from the old model based on land-intensive activities located on the outskirts of the large metropolis to the new model that promotes environmental quality in more distant parts of the region (but which pertain to the same market) is one of the key factors which will account for the higher growth and productivity levels in the proactive scenario.

Third, local economic policies that are targeted at the promotion of network economies. In the proactive scenario, the strategy based on the promotion of network economies is paramount. The aim is to intensify interdependence without needing to increase either urban size or proximity. The network nodes are interrelated and leave empty areas, preserving the environment, avoiding extensive use of territory. In short, the goal is to prevent urban sprawl.

This strategy requires the adoption of a cooperative and coordinated vision between cities and villages and local and regional authorities. The goal is to foster interdependence and to allow an increasingly diversified production in the whole region to preserve the specificities and productive specialization in different cities. This strategy is part of a recent proposal, based on the existence of a strong network of cities in Catalonia. This proposal, called 'Catalonia of cities' differs from the old proposal from the 1930s known as 'Catalonia-Ciutat'[2] in that it takes advantage of the network paradigm and does not focus on just one city. Catalonia of cities is devised in the context of a large transport infrastructure provision that provides an important part of the population with access to the services delivered along the network. The provision of specialized public services in the nodes is recommended to prevent the need for clones and fostering the emergence of scale economies, reducing the cost of delivery and increasing productivity.

Regarding network relationships of a private kind, the existence of productive network dynamics among agents located at distant nodes that could generate competitive advantages is assumed. It is possible to distinguish between 'synergy' networks and 'complementarity' networks. 'Synergy' network relationships arise between cities with similar production structures, increasing productivity in each of them as a result of the wider integrated activity scale. On the other hand, complementarity networks link different nodes with different areas production, allowing division of labour among them and wider markets for each one. Thus, coordinated endogenous development policies may increase the potential productivity growth rate of the whole province of Barcelona.

Local economic policies based on networks of cities are particularly useful in the field of R&D activities and higher or specialized education. Its implementation will result in significant savings in the provision of services and significant productivity gains in Catalonia as a whole and in the Barcelona province in particular.

---

[2]  The vision of Catalonia as just one city (*ciutat*) and in which Barcelona is only a neighbourhood in this city.

**Defensive scenario**

As a whole, the defensive scenario presupposes maintaining the same kind of production and not acting decisively with regard to transport infrastructure or to the conditions of supply (education and R&D). This means preserving or protecting small and poorly communicated labour markets, both in the rest of the metropolitan region and in the rest of the province.

## 10.3 SCENARIOS AND POLICIES AT THE INTRA-PROVINCE LEVEL

### 10.3.1 Growth Rates Estimation for Intra-Province Territories

On the basis of the three scenarios elaborated in this project and adapted in both quantitative and qualitative ways to the province of Barcelona, it is possible to make a quantitative forecast for the four intra-province sub-areas, namely the city of Barcelona, the rest of the metropolitan area, the Metropolitan Arc and the rest of the province. The methodology, funded on the use of a shift-share analysis, consists of three steps:

1. The GDP growth rate of the province in each scenario, given by the MAN-3 model, is converted to employment growth rate using the contribution of employment and productivity growth estimated for the region by the MASST model.[3]
2. In each sub-area the industry mix and the local competitive effect are calculated from its share and composition of employment in the previous period and adjusted on the basis of the international and local scenarios.
3. The sum of the three effects for each intra-province territory produces the expected employment growth rate for each scenario.

With regard to GDP in the Barcelona province (Table 10.1), the forecast annual growth rates are 2.89 per cent for the reference scenario, 3.96 per cent for the proactive scenario, and 1.88 per cent for the defensive scenario. The employment growth rate is 0.90 per cent for the reference scenario, 1.56 per cent for the proactive scenario, and 0.88 per cent for the defensive scenario.

---

[3] The assumption of similar regional (Catalonia) and province (Barcelona) contributions to employment and productivity growth rates is acceptable due to the large contribution of the province of Barcelona to Catalonian growth. The contributions come from the results of Chapters 4 and 5. The basis of the classic shift-share analysis is explained in Camagni (2005, pp. 152–4).

*Table 10.1    GDP, productivity and employment growth rates: Catalonia and Barcelona province (%)*

|  | 2001–2007* | Forecast 2010–2025 | | |
|---|---|---|---|---|
|  | Trend | Reference | Proactive | Defensive |
| *Catalonia* | | | | |
| Productivity growth rate | 0.77 | 2.09 | 2.41 | 1.09 |
| Employment growth rate | 3.20 | 0.95 | 1.60 | 0.97 |
| GDP growth rate | 3.97 | 3.06 | 4.05 | 2.07 |
| *Barcelona province* | | | | |
| Productivity growth rate | 0.64 | 1.97 | 2.36 | 0.99 |
| Employment growth rate | 3.16 | 0.90 | 1.56 | 0.88 |
| GDP growth rate | 3.80 | 2.89 | 3.96 | 1.88 |

*Note:*    * Based on INE-CRE.

*Source:*    Own elaboration.

The three scenarios suggest a positive growth rate of employment for every intra-province territory. However, the growth rates vary across territories and present a clear division between the proactive scenario and the other two.

In the reference scenario, the annual employment growth rate varies from 0.76 per cent in Barcelona city to 1.04 per cent in the Metropolitan Arc and 1 per cent in the rest of the province (Table 10.2). The province of Barcelona is still able to take advantage of agglomeration economies, labour force supply and exports, even if there is no transformation of its productive model. However, the consequences for productivity growth should be more apparent.

On the other hand, the proactive scenario suggests an employment growth rate between 60 and 80 per cent higher than the reference scenario. The city of Barcelona could grow at an annual growth rate of 1.4 per cent whereas the growth rates of the Metropolitan Arc (1.73 per cent), the rest of the province (1.7 per cent) and the metropolitan area without Barcelona (1.65 per cent) are quite similar.

Compared with the 2001–07 trend, the growth rates of employment are significantly lower. Barcelona grew at 2.2 per cent, the rest of the metropolitan area at 2.6 per cent, the Metropolitan Arc at 2.8 per cent, and the rest of the province at 2.8 per cent (Table 10.2). The slower growth of employment in the 2010–25 forecasts is due to the higher forecast contributions of productivity for GDP growth.

*Table 10.2     Annual employment 2010–2025 growth rates in the three scenarios (%)*

|  | 2001–2007 | Forecast annual growth rates 2010–2025 | | |
|---|---|---|---|---|
|  | Trend | Reference | Proactive | Defensive |
| Barcelona city (1) | 2.2 | 0.76 | 1.38 | 0.75 |
| Metropolitan area without Barcelona (2) | 2.6 | 0.97 | 1.65 | 0.94 |
| Metropolitan Arc (3) | 2.8 | 1.04 | 1.73 | 1.00 |
| Metropolitan region of Barcelona (1+2+3) | 2.4 | 0.89 | 1.55 | 0.87 |
| Rest of the province (4) | 2.8 | 1.00 | 1.70 | 1.02 |
| Total province (1+2+3+4) | 2.5 | 0.90 | 1.56 | 0.88 |

*Source:*   Own elaboration.

### 10.3.2   Policy Indications for the Intra-province Territories

Infrastructure policies will determine the new strategy for the whole territory of the Barcelona province. In particular, the transport, technological and educational infrastructure.

Regarding transport infrastructure, rail policies are fundamental, especially policies affecting the heart of the metropolis, and specifically accessibility to La Sagrera Station, which will become the core of the entire regional network, integrating the high-speed rail and regional rail transport. Similarly, the new orbital rail connection, linking Mataró and Vilanova i la Geltrú, through Granollers, Sabadell, Terrassa, Martorell and Vilafranca del Penedés, is intended to weave the network of cities into the whole Metropolitan Arc. Finally, the transversal axis linking Girona to Lleida, becomes crucial in joining the whole territory of the rest of the province of Barcelona; so it may be necessary to double the number of lanes on the existing motorway and then build the new high-speed rail line (Map 10.1. a–c).

Along with the rail infrastructure policy, a prominent role is occupied by policies intended to integrate the whole network of cities of the Barcelona province, with the aim of integrating their labour markets. Here the strategy is to help connect this network of cities through the promotion of knowledge-intensive activities, both locating new technological facilities and encouraging specialization in higher education. The goal is to promote the benefits of specialization of each node while promoting productive diversity in the whole system of cities.

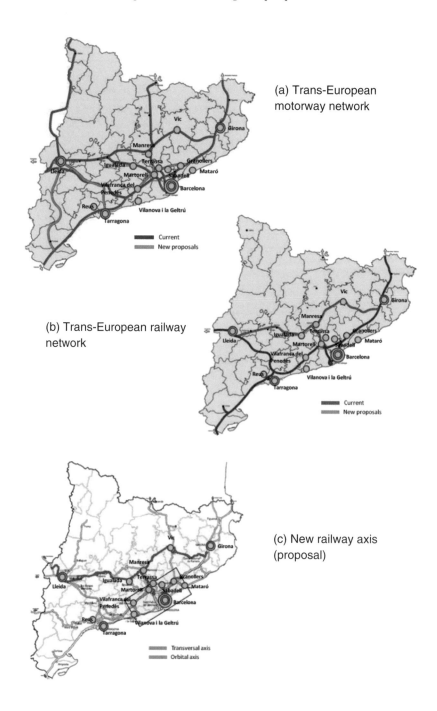

(a) Trans-European
motorway network

(b) Trans-European railway
network

(c) New railway axis
(proposal)

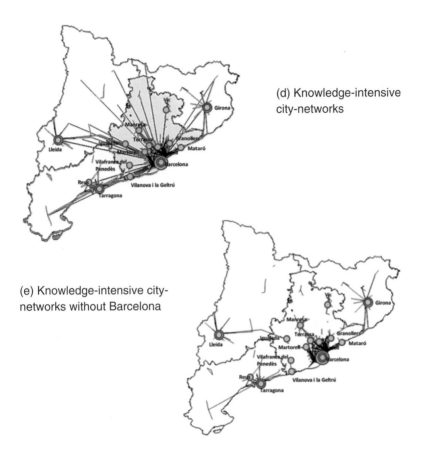

(d) Knowledge-intensive city-networks

(e) Knowledge-intensive city-networks without Barcelona

*Sources:* (a), (b) and (c): Generalitat de Catalunya; (d) and (e): Boix and Trullén (2007).

*Map 10.1 Infrastructure projects and knowledge-intensive city networks*

In any case, both the strategy of provision of transport infrastructure (particularly rail) as well as the strategy for provision of technological facilities or education, tend to complement each other, and to encourage a dynamic that favours the strengthening of economies of urbanization and localization, preventing the increasing trend to sprawl in the periphery and congestion in the centre.

In short, this intentional and proactive strategy is likely to enhance the competitiveness of all territories and especially of the nodes of the network which are more distant from the core cities of the metropolitan area. In

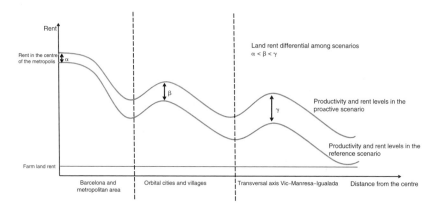

*Figure 10.1    A land rent model: differential effects of the scenarios on
              productivity, density and rent levels in the core and the two
              external rings of Barcelona province*

fact, when comparing the proactive with the reference scenario, productivity increases in the transversal axis cities, the most external inside the
province, will be higher than in the orbital cities and villages, and in the
orbital cities will be higher than in the metropolitan core. Of course, in
static terms, the closer these areas to the metropolitan core the higher the
level of absolute productivity. All these productivity elements are reflected
in GDP density and growth potential, and consequently are reflected in
the expected level of land rent (Figure 10.1).

The potential of these second- and third-rank centres to host advanced
activities is not just the outcome of wishful policies but is already present
*in nuce* in the territorial realm. In fact, it can be seen from Map 10.1
d–e, which depict the mobility of qualified people that many knowledge-
intensive interactions already occur between the secondary poles of the
province and the city of Barcelona, but also that a capability exists in
many of these poles to attract highly qualified employees: this is the case
in Granollers, Terrassa and Martorell, located along the proposed orbital
rail network and, more externally, in Girona, Manresa and Lleida, which
will be affected by the new infrastructure projects.

Map 10.2 summarizes the economic and territorial development strategy introduced in the proactive scenario (on the background of the map,
the forecast growth rates of the Catalan provinces have already been mentioned in Section 10.3). Its main elements are:

1.   Integration of long-distance transportation axes, large metropolitan
     transportation axes, linking main sub-centres of the province, and

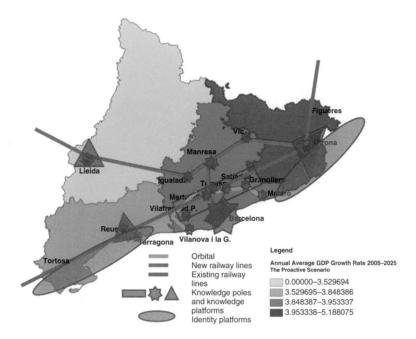

*Map 10.2    Policy strategies for Barcelona province*

local territories, through what we call 'Transport platforms'. New transport infrastructure has to integrate territories – in a functional, physical, environmental and visual way – in order to represent multi-dimensional assets for a new *aménagement du territoire*.

2.  The existence of a large central polarity in Barcelona and in the Metropolitan Area of Barcelona (MAB – 36 municipalities). Note that the increasing number of knowledge-intensive activities will expand from the central municipality of Barcelona – which will obviously remain the crucial knowledge pole of the region – towards all the 36 contiguous municipalities of the metropolitan area. The knowledge pole will expand towards a 'territorial knowledge platform'. The population is approximately 3.2 million inhabitants.

3.  The creation of a Metropolitan Arc around the MAB defined by the cities of Mataró, Granollers, Sabadell, Terrassa, Martorell and Vilafranca del Penedès i Vilanova i La Geltrú, which is linked by the new orbital railway line. This arc accounts for around 1.8 million inhabitants. Productivity increases will be higher than in the central metropolitan area, thanks to the attraction and development of new advanced, knowledge-intensive activities.

4.  The central role of the Vic, Manresa and Igualada poles is crucial for the transversal axis built around high-speed train and road infrastructure.
5.  Three cities providing equilibrium in Catalonia outside the Barcelona province, enlarging the development of the central metropolis: Girona-Costa Brava, Reus-Tarragona and Lleida. These metropolises are called 'knowledge platforms'; integrating territories organize themselves well beyond the single cities and benefit both from externalities supplied by these surrounding territories – landscape amenities, environmental quality, infrastructure – and by the presence of the Barcelona core.

On the outskirts of traditional tourist areas (Costa Brava–Girona and Costa Daurada–Tarragona) new developments occur with a growing number of knowledge-intensive services, attracting a European population on a permanent or semi-permanent basis. A trend will emerge from tourism to permanent or semi-permanent activity location, attracted by the high quality of life, similar to what is already taking place on the coast of Barcelona province and in other coastal areas of the Latin Arc. The appeal will largely be derived from local specificities: the cultural heritage of traditional centres, the enhanced quality of the landscape, the sea, the easy access to a lively city such as Barcelona, the renewed cultural life in second- and third-rank cities – what we call 'identity platforms'.

The Granollers–Martorell axis becomes the new main 'knowledge corridor' of the Catalan economy, with the location of the headquarters of large technological Catalan and Spanish firms, of multinational corporations and also of important university centres such as, for instance, the Universitat Autònoma de Barcelona (awarded the distinction of 'International Campus of Excellence' by the Spanish government).

Note that in the proactive scenario, the growth of the Barcelona metropolis does not take place in an empty periphery. In fact the opposite is true: the Vic–Manresa–Igualada axis and the technological Metropolitan Arc (the knowledge corridor) will have a different impact on the growth of the outskirts of the metropolis whether the proactive scenario strategy is implemented or not. In fact, stimulating a networked poly-centricity through the location of high-productivity activities means a completely new territorial growth model with respect to the traditional metropolitan model based on centrifugal forces that generically expand from the central core towards peripheries.

Thus, the whole metropolis will show higher levels of productivity growth compared to the reference scenario and consequently economic growth will be higher.

# References

Affuso, A., R. Capello and U. Fratesi (2011), 'Globalization and competitive strategies in European vulnerable regions', *Regional Studies*, **45** (5), 657–75.

Aghion, P. and E. Cohen (2004), 'Education et Croissance', *La Documentation française*, Paris.

ArcoLatino (2010), http://www.arcolatino.org/index.php?lng=2.

Aschauer, D. (1989), 'Is public expenditure productive?', *Journal of Monetary Economics*, **23** (2), 177–200.

Barro, R.J. (2001), 'Human capital and growth', *American Economic Review*, **91** (2), 12–17.

Boix, R. (2006), 'Las Áreas Metropolitanas en España', XXXII Reunión de Estudios Regionales, Ourense, 16–28 November.

Boix, R. and V. Galletto (2004), 'Anàlisi Econòmica Comparada del Cens de 2001. Principals Resultats per a Catalunya', *Nota de Economia*, no. 7, ISSN: 0213-3640.

Boix, R. and V. Galletto (2006), 'Sistemas Locales de Trabajo y Distritos Industriales Marshallianos en España', *Economía Industrial*, no. 359, 165–84.

Boix, R. and J. Trullén (2007), 'Knowledge, networks of cities and growth in regional urban systems', *Papers in Regional Science*, **86** (4), 551–74.

Boix, R. and J. Trullén (2010), 'La Relevancia Empírica de los Distritos Industriales Marshallianos y los Sistemas Productivos Locales Manufactureros de Gran Empresa en España', IERMB Working Paper in Economics, no. 10.01, January.

Boix, R. and P. Veneri (2009), 'Metropolitan areas in Spain and Italy', IERMB Working Paper in Economics, no. 09.01, March.

Camagni, R. (1993), 'From city hierarchy to city network: reflections about an emerging paradigm', in T.R. Lakshmanan and P. Nijkamp (eds), *Structure and Change in the Space Economy, Festschrift in honor of Martin Beckmann*, Berlin: Springer Verlag, pp. 66–87.

Camagni, R. (2002), 'On the concept of territorial competitiveness: sound or misleading?', *Urban Studies*, **39** (13), 2395–411.

Camagni, R. (2005), *Economia Urbana*, Barcelona: Antoni Bosch, editor S.A.

Camagni, R. (2009), 'Territorial capital and regional development', in

R. Capello and P. Nijkamp (eds), *Handbook in Regional Growth and Development Theories*, Cheltenham, UK and Northampton, MA, USA: Edward Elgar, pp. 118–32.

Camagni, R. and R. Capello (2004), 'The city network paradigm: theory and empirical evidence', in R. Capello and P. Nijkamp (eds), *Urban Dynamics and Growth: Advances in Urban Economics*, Amsterdam: Elsevier, pp. 495–532.

Camagni, R. and R. Capello (2009), 'Territorial capital and regional competitiveness: theory and evidence', *Studies in Regional Science*, **39** (1), 19–40.

Camagni, R. and R. Capello (2010), 'Macroeconomic and territorial policies for regional competitiveness: an EU perspective', *Regional Science Policy and Practice*, **2** (1) 1–19.

Camagni, R. and D. Maillat (eds) (2006), *Milieux Innovateurs: Théorie et Politiques*, Paris: Economica.

Camagni, R. and C. Salone (1993), 'Network urban structures in northern Italy: elements for a theoretical framework', *Urban Studies*, **30** (6), 1053–64.

Capello, R. (2007), 'A forecasting territorial model of regional growth: the MASST model', *Annals of Regional Science*, **41** (4), 753–87.

Capello, R. and U. Fratesi (2009), 'Modelling European regional scenarios: aggressive versus defensive competitive strategies', *Environment and Planning A*, **4** (2), 481–504.

Capello, R., R. Camagni, B. Chizzolini and U. Fratesi (2008), *Modelling Regional Scenarios for the Enlarged Europe: European Competitiveness and Global Strategies*, Berlin: Springer-Verlag.

Capello, R., U. Fratesi and L. Resmini (2011), *Globalization and Regional Growth in Europe: Past Trends and Future Scenarios*, Berlin: Springer-Verlag.

CEC (Commission of the European Communities) (2004), *Foresight and the Transition to Regional Knowledge-Based Economies*, Synthesis Report, DG for Research Information and Communication Unit, Brussels.

CEC (Commission of the European Communities) (2005), 'Europe 2020', Brussels.

CEC (Commission of the European Communities) (2007), *Growing Regions, Growing Europe*, Fourth Report on Economic and Social Cohesion, Brussels.

CEC (Commission of the European Communities) (2010), 'Europe 2020', Brussels.

Clusa, J. and J. Roca (1997), 'El Canvi d'escala de la Ciutat Metropolitana de Barcelona', *Revista Econòmica de Catalunya*, no. 33, 44–53.

ESPON Project EDORA (2010), 'European Development Opportunities for Rural Areas', Final Report.

Forni, M. and S. Paba (2000), 'The sources of local growth: evidence from Italy', *Giornale degli Economisti e Annali di Economia*, **59** (1), 1–49.

Hawkins, J. (2001), 'Economic forecasting: history and procedures', mimeo available at: http://www.treasury.gov.au/documents/987/PDF/02_eco_forecasting.pdf.

Hendry, D. and M.P. Clements (2001), 'Economic forecasting: some lessons from recent research', mimeo available at: http://economics.ouls.ox.ac.uk/11973/1/ecbwp082.pdf.

Holl, A. (2004), 'Manufacturing location and impacts of road transport infrastructure: empirical evidence from Spain', *Regional Science and Urban Economics*, **34** (3), 341–63.

Kaldor, N. (1970), 'The case of regional policies', *Scottish Journal of Political Economy*, **17** (3), 337–48.

Loomis, D.G. and J.E. Cox Jr (2000), 'A course in economic forecasting: rationale and content', *Journal of Economic Education*, **31** (4), 349–57.

Lucas, R.E. (1988), 'On the mechanics of economic development', *Journal of Monetary Economics*, **22** (1), 3–42.

Miles, I. and M. Keenan (2000), 'Foren Issue Paper. From National to Regional Foresight: Experiences and Methods', workshop 1, Manchester, April.

Myrdal, G. (1957), *Economic Theory of Underdeveloped Regions*, London: Gerald Duckworth.

Nelson, R.R. and E.S. Phelps (1966), 'Investment in humans, technological diffusion and economic growth', *American Economic Review*, **56** (2), March, 69–75.

OECD (2001), *Territorial Outlook*, Paris: OECD.

OECD (2006), *Competitive Cities in the Global Economy*, Paris: OECD.

OECD (2008), *Economic Survey of Spain*, Paris: OECD.

OECD (2009a), *OECD Rural Policy Review: Spain*, Paris: OECD.

OECD (2009b), *Economic Survey of France*, Paris: OECD

OECD (2009c), *Economic Survey of Italy*, Paris: OECD.

Perloff, H. (1957), 'Interrelations of state income and industrial structure', *Review of Economics and Statistics*, **39** (2), 162–71.

Perloff, H., E. Dunn, E. Lampard and R. Muth (1960), *Region, Resources and Economic Growth*, Baltimore, MD: Johns Hopkins University Press.

Putnam, R.D. (1993), *Making Democracy Work: Civic Traditions in Modern Italy*, Princeton, NJ: Princeton University Press.

Richardson, H.W. (1969), *Regional Economics*, World University, Trowbridge, UK: Redwood Press.

Roca, J., M. Burns and M. Moix (2005), 'Las Áreas Metropolitanas

Españolas. Evolución 1991–2001', Centro de Política del Suelo y Valoraciones, Universitat de Catalunia, Barcelona (mimeo).

Salvador, N., C. Mora and E. Salvat (1997), 'La Regió Urbana Funcional de Barcelona en el Context Europeu', *Revista Econòmica de Catalunya*, no. 33.

Torrero, A.M. (2009), 'La Crisis Financiera Internacional. Repercusión Sobre la Economía Española', Documentos de Trabajo Instituto Universitario de Análisis Económico y Social, 98/09, Universidad de Alcalà.

Trullén, J. (2000), 'Economia de la Barcelona Metropolitana', in R. Gomà and Joan Subirats (eds), *Govern i Polítiques Públiques a Catalunya*, Barcelona: Ariel, pp. 131–4.

Trullén, J. and R. Boix (2000), 'Policentrismo y Redes de Ciudades en la Región Metropolitana de Barcelona', paper presented at the Third Congreso de Economía Aplicada, Universitat de Valencia, 1–3 June.

Trullén, J. and R. Boix (2006), 'Anàlisi Econòmica del Centre de la Regió Metropolitana da Barcelona: Economia del pla Estratègic Metropolità de Barcelona', Elements de Debat Territorial, Diputació de Barcelona, Barcelona.

Trullén, J. and R. Boix (2008), 'Knowledge externalities and networks of cities in creative metropolis', in P. Cooke and L. Lazzeretti (eds), *Creative Cities, Cultural Clusters and Local Economic Development*, Cheltenham, UK and Northampton, MA, USA: Edward Elgar, pp. 211–37.

UNCTAD (2009), *World Investment Report 2009: Transnational Corporations, Agricultural Production and Development*, United Nations Conference on Trade and Development, New York and Geneva: UNCTAD.

UNIDO (2004), *Foresight Methodologies*, United Nations Industrial Development Organisation, Vienna: UNIDO.

Wegener, M., H. Eskelinnen, F. Fürst, C. Schürmann and K. Spiekermann (2002), 'Criteria for the spatial differentiation of the EU territory: geographical position', Forschungen 102.2, Bundesamt für Bauwesen und Raumordnung, Bonn.

# Index